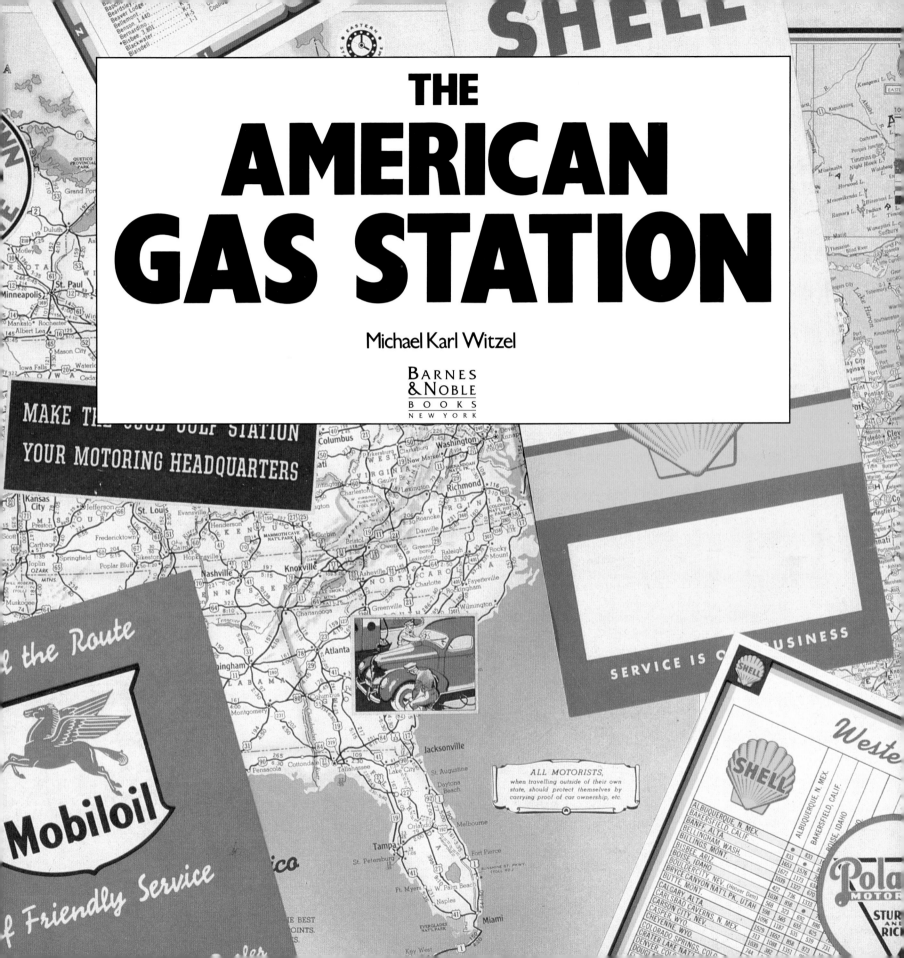

THE
AMERICAN
GAS STATION

Michael Karl Witzel

BARNES
&NOBLE
BOOKS
NEW YORK

For Karl, Gabriele and Gyvel;
like the classic gas stations
that lined America's roadsides,
you were always there when needed.

This edition published by Barnes & Noble, Inc., by arrangement with MBI Publishing Company.

1999 Barnes & Noble Books

M 10 9 8 7 6 5 4 3 2

ISBN 0-7607-1240-9

First published in 1992 by MBI Publishing Company

Library of Congress Cataloging-in-Publication Data Available

On the front cover: Socony's Pegasus was adopted as the company's trademark shortly after the organization of Socony-Vacuum in 1931. By the heyday of the American gas station in the 1950s, the red flying horse was omnipresent on American streets and omnipotent in people's minds as the symbol for gasoline. This Pegasus is from a small radiator mascot distributed to motorists at gas stations circa 1950. *Michael Karl Witzel*

On the frontispiece: Ethyl magazine advertisement from 1953 with a gas pump portrayed as a skyscraper ruling over the traffic at its feet.

On the contents page: Sinclair Opaline motor oil. With an early version of the company's mascot, Dino. Sinclair's oils were advertised as "Mellowed 80 Million Years" in 1934. *Atlantic Richfield Company*

Printed in Hong Kong

Contents

Acknowledgments

Without the support and encouragement of certain individuals, this project would have never left the station. I would like to thank the countless people who helped shape the direction of this book during its beginnings, with special credit going to James Bettes for his important leads on interesting locations and important initial contacts. Also, thanks to Tash Matsuoka and *Rider* magazine for their interest in gasoline pumps and to Bob Walters and the staff at the Main Station for believing in the concept during its early stages. Special recognition is reserved for Loy P. Sturch and Jennifer Tomlinson for their early insights and directions.

A number of individuals, organizations and businesses also worked behind the scenes to make this book a reality, including Joan Johnson and the detectives at Circa Research & Reference, Gabriele Witzel and Documentation Support, Lynn Mayes and the Black & White Works, Al Yadao and the staff at Reproductions, the Color Place, Prolab, the Tucson Public Library, the Arizona Historical Society, the International Petroliana Collectors Association, the Society for Commercial Archeology, the Historic Route 66 Association of Arizona, the Historical Society of King County, the National Archives and the Library of Congress.

Appreciative kudos go to Gyvel Z. Young for her continuing support and editorial suggestions, Michael Yorks for his logical proofreading of station interviews during lunch-break sessions at the Lazy B, and Wolfram Streiff for his indirect sponsorship and support of the project. My sincerest gratitude goes to the long list of petroleum refiners and gasoline pump manufacturers who assisted with historical information and archival photography, including company representatives Judith Ashelin, Ken Catlin, Marjorie C. Federici, Kathy Holland, Mary C. Keane, Dottie McKenna, Marsha L. Meyer, Robert B. Finney and David LeBeau.

I would also like to acknowledge the numerous petroliana collectors and highway aficionados who answered queries promptly and helped to locate specific photographs and petroliana artifacts. Jeffrey Pedersen was an invaluable help with the formulation of historical anecdotes, and the General Petroleum Museum collection in Seattle was more than adequate for gathering specific photographic images.

In addition, my thanks are directed to Warren Anderson, Will Anderson, Jerry Chinn, Don Eager, Frederick G. Frost, Jr., Gasoline Gus Garton, Clarence Goodburn, Vic Huber, Ed Love, Mike Parsons, Keith A. Sculle, Larry Shirkey, Guy Spangenburg, Shelly Steichen, Edward L. Wesemann, Jr., and all the other contributors who are in some way involved with the preservation of the great American gas station.

Michael K. Witzel

Clare Patterson shows off a prized can of Gargoyle-brand motor oil in front of his backyard station in a private village he calls Pattersonville, USA. Inside his replica station building, a wide array of petroliana delights are on display to the hundreds of nostalgia-happy visitors attending his yearly backyard picnics.

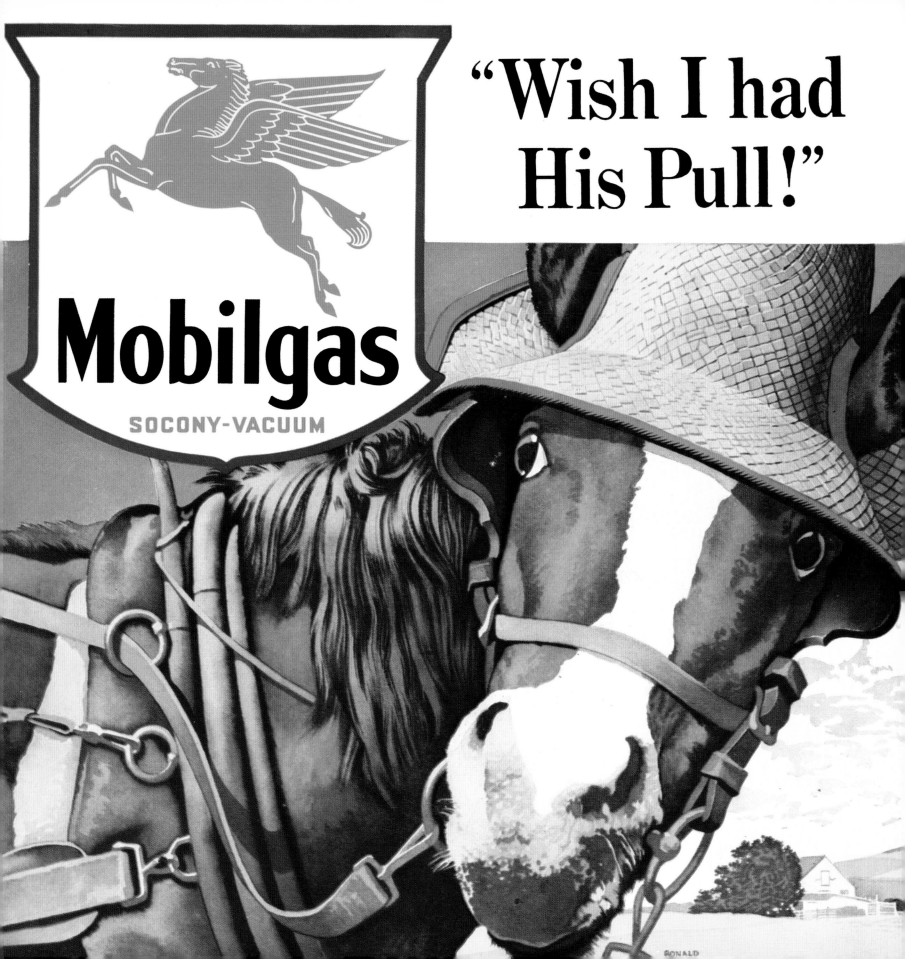

Foreword

As we vanguards of the baby boom generation enter into the middle age plateau of life and reach our peak earning years with ample discretionary income, we are seeking something more. What started out as a barely perceptible murmur has now grown into a swell of enthusiasm for the happy times of our long-ago youth. We yearn for the simpler times when life wasn't so harried and the pace was slower—a time in this country when a handshake meant something and people cared about other people.

Vintage automobiles, American Flyer sleds, bright red pedal cars—these are some of the catalysts that take us back on mental journeys to our happy days long gone, days when old Grandpop's eyes twinkled as he demonstrated the Lionel train set he received for Christmas as a kid or showed us how to cast his favorite fishing pole at the local swimming hole. As life becomes more complex, these simple memories become more important.

Interest in nostalgia is at an all-time high in the United States, with many Americans joining the craze to collect, hoard and purchase one-of-a-kind artifacts from yesteryear. Nostalgic associations of all types abound, including Coca-Cola memorabilia collectors, groups fond of paper and sign advertising, muscle car clubs and, yes, even organizations devoted to the memorabilia once taken for granted as part of the filling station businesses of another era.

The profiles within this book are about the real people who gave meaning to those lifeless objects, unique gas station proprietors involved in their own individual way with the refueling of America's automobiles. All had the freedom to dream their own dream and create a life of their choosing, in the process making a personal contribution to the big picture. With automobile transportation as their common denominator, all shared a kinship in the realm of the gasoline refueling station.

In this book, Michael K. Witzel captures the essence of these interesting and colorful petroleum people, including glimpses of gasoline structures and artifacts taken from the simpler days when caring individuals made a difference and service was still the rule. As in his regular column for *Check the Oil!* magazine, he carries a unique perspective forward into this writing, celebrating the glorious, golden days of service to the automobile. By doing so, he not only enlightens the reader to many interesting facts, but permanently documents an integral part of our cultural heritage: the American gas station.

Jerry Keyser
Editor and Publisher of Check the Oil! *magazine*
Box 1000, Westerville, Ohio 43081
June 1991

Mobil magazine advertisement from 1940. The Big Brown Horse is envious for more than one reason: the Flying Red Horse not only had more pull but also had powered the horseless carriages that would eventually replace it.

Chapter 1

Birth of the American Filling Station, 1898-1907

Before the dawn of the Twentieth Century, when only a handful of Charles E. and J. Frank Duryea's one-cylinder horseless carriages were roaming the countryside and Alexander Winton's first series-produced gas buggies were initially sold, locating liquid fuel to power their simple engines was difficult. In those pioneering days of the gasoline engine, automobile refueling stations situated for motorcar operators to pull into and refill their gas tanks didn't exist. Pumping a tank full of gasoline was a task far removed from the simplicity and convenience of today's modern service station.

Kerosene was unchallenged as the primary fluid refined by major oil companies for commercial sale. Burning cleaner than whale oil and with more efficiency, this "coal oil" was the sole source of illumination for many. Because a gallon of kerosene sold for twice as much as a barrel of crude oil, petroleum refiners made large profits by its manufacture. After the refining process, one barrel of crude oil yielded more than forty percent gasoline and only three percent kerosene, creating large quantities of waste gasoline for disposal.

That Nuisance Gas

Small amounts of this unwanted gasoline were retained and burned in special cookstoves built just for the purpose and in special lamps designed for the illumination of city streets.

Unfortunately, commercial uses ultimately proved dangerous, and it wasn't long before the highly explosive properties of this nuisance fluid limited its sale as fuel for cooking or illumination. With its higher margin of safety, kerosene was much more popular than the accidentally discovered waste byproduct known as stove naptha. Since the market required for gasoline's profitability didn't exist, the selling and distribution of this fuel remained limited.

The genius of Thomas Edison was only beginning to illuminate the lives of millions dependent upon kerosene and natural gas for light. Until his 1882 invention of the light bulb could be coupled with the perfection of the economical production-line motorcar, oil companies had no choice but to keep the refinement of kerosene high. No one could foresee that kerosene's consumption would one day pale in comparison with the demand for gasoline—once the full effects of the automobile age made its impact known throughout the towns and villages of the states.

By the end of 1899, transportation by motorcar struggled in its infancy, with the great quantity of vehicle sales still a decade away. It was only a few months since Henry Ford had left his post as chief engineer for the Edison Electric Plant in Detroit and with a group of investors formed his first automobile manufacturing company. Still in its early experimentation

Wingspout one-quart copper oil dispenser. With this interesting device, the spout is pulled downward and put into the oil refilling opening of an automobile. Filled with one quart of oil, the copper container then empties into the crankcase.

Charles Duryea installed the first set of pneumatic tires on this one-cylinder converted buggy on March 11, 1895. Utilizing a tiller control for steering, it was an unusual sight for people accustomed to the horse and carriage mode of transportation. In those pioneering days of the gasoline engine, there were no automobile refueling stations situated for the convenience of motorcar operators to pull into and refill their gas tanks. The street scene at this time was still dominated by the horse-drawn carriage and wooden-spoke wheels. Still in its early experimental stages, the economical motorcar for the masses was only a dream on paper. The thirty other American automobile manufacturers already in production only turned out an estimated 2,500 motor vehicles. Sold to a very restricted audience, these expensive automobiles limited horseless transportation to a small segment of society. *Oil & Gas Journal*

stages, the economical motorcar for the masses was only a dream. The thirty other American automobile manufacturers already in production turned out only an estimated 2,500 motor vehicles. Sold to a restricted audience, these expensive automobiles limited horseless transportation to a small segment of society.

Regarded as a novelty reserved for those rich enough to purchase one, the automobile was principally owned by doctors, lawyers and the upper elite of society. The horse and buggy provided personal locomotion for a large majority of the general public, and the newfangled invention known as the horseless carriage was looked upon as a status symbol for those with money to waste. Many hoped this "hobby" of the well-to-do would die a slow death, like many fads before it. Most could not conceive that this mechanical contrivance would ever replace the four-footed equine, still much adored for transportation.

The Bulk Outlet Gas Oasis

In these early days, filling a motor vehicle with the precious liquid required for a carefree weekend jaunt demanded careful planning. Because gasoline pumping devices were still to be invented, perfected and manufactured, an intimate knowledge of where to obtain the combustible fuel needed to keep one's vehicle in motion was a prerequisite to any sort of extended travel. This wasn't as easy as it sounded, since gasoline for the unproven motorcar was available at only a smattering of locations. The profusion of curb pumps and organized system of service stations to follow were not yet conceived in the minds of the period's automobile architects.

The nation's roadway system was also in a sorry state; the few dirt corridors available for overland travel were barely passable in most locations. Ninety percent of available roads were still unpaved, and transportation from the city to the country and back again was designed for the wooden-spoke wheels of the horse-drawn carriage, period. Those wishing to go against this established and accepted method of travel had to make do with the conveniences available. In the minds of a few adventurous people, the idea of motoring from coast to coast existed only as a possibility.

Early refueling outposts known as bulk depots served as crude gasoline sales outlets for the infrequent oddity of the horseless carriage. Located outside highly populated areas, these depots generally merchandised the liquid in cans and other bulk containers. The specialized equipment required for safe and efficient refueling of automobiles had not been designed, so vehicle owner and depot operator had to manage with contrivances designed for other purposes. Consequently, the process of purchasing gasoline required a number of steps unheard of at today's modern gasoline station. For the new motorist, it wasn't hard to see that pouring a highly flammable liquid down the small opening of a machine that sputtered and smoked was something the bulk depot operator was ill prepared for.

Because of the limited number of bulk businesses in operation before the twenties, enthusiastic automobile owners had to rely on their own wits and ingenuity to keep their vehicles going for extended distances. As the gaps between fuel outlets were far, motorists were often towed the last few miles to a fuel depot by a sympathetic horse and buggy owner. Unlike the motorcar, the horse consumed grass for its power, and its fuel was available near the side of

At the early bulk depot, gasoline was often transferred from five-gallon containers into a handheld pitcher used to pour it into a large chamois-covered funnel. Here, an extra stage was added to the procedure by utilizing a filtration contraption precariously positioned on the automobile's running board. Since it often required three people to refuel a gas tank, more efficient methods of dispensing gasoline would have to be developed before the motorcar could gain wide acceptance from the public. *Arizona Historical Society, Tucson*

any roadway—much to the chagrin of the embarrassed horseless age neophyte.

The Dangers of Smoking

Gasoline was often stored in a cylindrical steel drum at the bulk establishments, perched high atop a wooden timber support structure or raised stone base. From this precarious storage container, unfiltered gasoline flowed from a valve-controlled spout into a tin measuring can capable of holding five gallons or less of fluid.

Once properly measured, the gasoline was poured by hand from this container, with great care, through a large metal funnel held by a helpful motorist or depot employee. To trap sediment and filter out any foreign particles that might damage an automobile engine, this homemade instrument was frequently covered with chamois cloth. Ever so slowly, gasoline trickled through this leather filtration stage,

13

In 1911, the Standard Oil Company operated this Ohio refueling stop offering its complete line of Zerolene and Polarine lubricants to the motoring public. Though it was a dangerous place to work, even the youngest laborers helped out if they could, with the familiar refueling can and funnel always ready to service a vehicle that might stop in. Gassing up an automobile back then was basic, with the added luxury of drive-up pumps and curbside service rare. *Standard Oil Company*

quickly chugging the final few inches through the funnel spout into the hungry automobile's depleted fuel tank.

Because fuel gauges weren't employed in the first automotive vehicles, sight and sound had to serve for determining fuel level. The bulk operator filling a vehicle's tank could see the amount of gas accumulating by peering straight down the auto's refilling tube and a decision on whether or not the tank was full had to be made visually. When the filler neck was curved, an experienced ear had to be cocked near the inlet to measure the increasing fluid volume aurally. When an occasional air pocket formed in the tube, which frequently occurred, the hapless tank refiller often received a splash of gasoline right in the ear.

Of course, gasoline also flowed unintentionally onto a variety of other surfaces, resulting in soiled clothing, stained hands and dirty surroundings. But that was the least of one's worries. During any one of the laborious measuring and filling steps, a spark or open flame within range of these combustible fumes could easily ignite the volatile vapors without warning.

Storage of peripheral refueling materials was extremely dangerous, too. Highly combustible refilling cans, funnels with gasoline-soaked chamois and the various cleanup rags used during the refueling process had to be stocked somewhere for their next use. This, as well as other obvious safety drawbacks, gave the bulk refueling depot a dangerous reputation, accounting for its location far away from densely inhabited areas—usually on the outer fringes of urban population centers. Still, many tragic accidents occurred, resulting in horrific explosions and fires, adding nothing to further the cause of the latter-day drivers and their supposedly modern machines.

Motoring for the Fun of It

Fortunately, motoring enthusiasts weren't deterred by the dangers as widespread excitement for the automobile continued to be engendered by a number of highly publicized events. Ransom E. Olds kicked off the excitement in the fall of 1901 when he decided to have his factory tester, Roy D. Chapin, drive a brand-new curved-dash Oldsmobile from his Detroit manufacturing plant to the upcoming automobile show in New York City. The one-cylinder, tiller-steered vehicle that sold for a mere $650 had no problem making the trip—even if it was basically a modified surrey carriage with a motorized engine.

Transcontinental motor tours featuring a plethora of competing automobile manufacturers and their economical vehicles soon followed. Dr. H. Nelson Jackson embarked on his own promotional journey when he crossed the entire American continent accompanied by his chauffeur in 1903. Driving a brand-new Winton motorcar, the adventuresome pair took only sixty-three days to make the overland journey from downtown San Francisco to the streets of New York City without major incident or breakdown.

Gradually, the average motorist became less worried about the reliability of the automobile and the availability of the gasoline that powered it. By the end of the 1800s, new-car sales slowly picked up momentum, and at the turn of the century, more than 8,000 vehicles were registered in the United States, including cars and trucks. The year 1904 saw several thousand progressive Americans abandoning provincial modes of travel to take yearly vacations in an exciting new automobile. The notion of long-distance automotive touring had been officially established, the viability and practicality of the motorcar acknowledged.

To keep pace with the growing demand to refuel these new vehicles, wholesale jobbers began to transport gasoline in horsedrawn tank trucks to commercial customers in town, who stored and sold fuel in small quantities. Prefilled tin containers holding one gallon or less could now be stocked for sale like any other product; the automobile repair garages and storage facilities that were proliferating throughout the nation finally had a way to keep gasoline supplies available. In conjunction with the general store, druggist, bicycle shop and livery stable that also sold fuel, these new gasoline sellers helped decrease the reliance on the bulk depot.

Yet the same "drum-and-measure" methods practiced at the first bulk refueling depots

The development of the
American gasoline station
reached an exciting new
level of progress by 1905
when the Automobile
Gasoline Company was
formed by Harry Grenner
and Clem Laessig in St.
Louis, Missouri. By utilizing
a gravity fed tank and the
revolutionary addition of a
simple garden hose, the
inventive duo opened for
business what many
historians agree constituted
America's first real "filling"
station. Grenner and
Laessig were on to
something big—and they
knew it. They continued
their initial success by
opening stations
throughout St. Louis until
they had a chain of forty
outlets. *Shell Oil Company*

continued to be followed at these new retail gas
outposts. The small improvements made in the
availability of motor fuel continued to be eclipsed
by an inherent lack of safe and practical refueling methods. But, like the latest automobile
models, these methods were soon to change for
the better. Fully equipped gasoline stations pos-
sessing all the modern accouterments demanded by the ever-expanding market of
automobile consumers were only a few years
away. The gasoline age had officially begun, and

all of the United States was soon to be behind the
wheel.

The Lowly Garden Hose

The development of the American gasoline
station reached an exciting new level of progress
by 1905 when the Automobile Gasoline Company was formed by Harry Grenner and Clem
Laessig in St. Louis. Starting primarily in the
business as bulk fuel distributors with huge
above-ground storage tanks, the shrewd part-

Contemplating some 300 horseless carriages scurrying across the downtown streets of Seattle inspired John McLean to design and build what he called a "filling station" and he began to serve the fifteen cars per day that eagerly pulled in. *Museum of History and Industry, Seattle*

In the early days of motoring, automobiles came without any sort of fuel gauge. This left the vehicle owner sometimes stranded by the roadside without gasoline. To counter the problem, companies like King-Seeley manufactured add-on Tele-gauges touted by engineering experts as "the most accurate and dependable solution to the problem."

nership calculated that overall income could increase by offering gasoline for sale to motorists in a quick, efficient and practical manner.

By installing a gravity-fed tank resembling an oversized water heater and attaching an ordinary garden hose to its base, the inventive duo opened America's first real "gas station." Finally, the drum-and-measure system had been eliminated. Now, a simple gauge replaced the metal containers formerly used for gasoline measurement. The funnel and chamois were dropped too, as the revolutionary flexible garden hose performed the job with more accuracy and less spillage.

Finally, the station operator's job was one step easier, the once tedious task of topping off a gas tank greatly simplified. Controlled by a hand-operated valve, gasoline now flowed through a simple filtration system installed in-line as an integral part of the entire tank feed unit. All an employee had to do was stick the end of the hose into an automobile tank's filler neck and let the fuel flow freely. Laessig and Grenner were on to something big, and they knew it, continuing their initial success by opening stations throughout St. Louis until a small chain of forty outlets plus one depot was organized.

Operations similar to the American Gasoline Company outlets began to spring up around the country with regular frequency. Standard Oil of California (Socal) followed Laessig and Gren-

Gulf Refining Company utilized tank wagons drawn by a team of horses to deliver kerosene to the countless businesses that sold it during the early 1900s. Because merchants often recognized brands by the color of the tank wagon, Gulf colored its orange after discovering the hue wasn't used by any other refiners. Later, this color was adopted on a companywide scale and utilized in the Sign of the Orange Disk. *Chevron Corporation*

ner's lead in 1907 with its first of many drive-in filling stations organized on the West Coast.

John McLean, Socal area sales manager for the new Seattle territory, was inspired one day when contemplating some 300 horseless carriages scurrying across the downtown streets of Seattle. With just the right marketing approach, McLean was sure that the imaginations—and pocketbooks—of this burgeoning market of gasoline buyers could easily be captured and ultimately influenced to patronize a refueling station of his own personal design.

Initiating his new ideas without delay, McLean secured a small site on Holgate Street just off the busy Alaskan Way and mounted an upright cylindrical thirty gallon tank on a wooden post. A simple valve controlled the tank's gravity flow, with a flexible hose attached to its base intended for refilling automobiles without fuss. When the small storage receptable emptied, the gasoline supply could easily be replenished with new fuel stock by way of a convenient connection to the nearby Standard Oil Company feeder tank located at the bulk plant across the street.

McLean dubbed his streetside brain child a "filling station" and began to serve the fifteen cars per day that eagerly pulled in. Gasoline was now being served—one hurried customer at a time. Mounted next to the gasoline storage tank, a No Smoking sign and shelving for the display of Standard's Zerolene and Polarine brands of grease and oil were two of the new features McLean felt were necessary. Now, ancillary petroleum products could easily be seen by all who drove up, accounting for what probably was the first point-of-purchase display at a filling station. This turned out to be a visionary move, as tires, batteries and accessories would constitute a large portion of service station income in the upcoming years.

As all the elements of McLean's design came together, the public welcomed the ease of driving up and having their motorcars refilled with speed and efficiency. Before long, more than 200 vehicles per day lined up on Holgate Street just to take advantage of McLean's advanced methods of dispensing gasoline fuel.

The creative rearrangement of simple elements already existing in other forms made his station a runaway success. The concept of a drive-in gas station was confirmed by the patronage of many enthusiastic motorists. Closer than ever to achieving its ultimate form, the filling station was poised to take its rightful place on almost every street corner in the new motoring America.

Bowser: A Motorist's Best Friend

When the craze for the automobile was first beginning to show signs of becoming an unstoppable movement in the early 1900s, automotive enthusiasts realized that without practical machinery to put gas into their flivver's tank, this newfound mode of transportation would soon become extinct.

The automobile of the early 1900s had a tendency to make funny noises after a certain time, especially the surrey-style buggies, which usually rattled apart after a short time. Just as gasoline additives are important to the car owner today, squeak remedies were held in high esteem by the vehicle owner of yesteryear. Just a drop on dirt-bound spring leaves and your troubles were over—no more embarrassing squeaks.

S. F. Bowser & Company manufactured a variety of gasoline pumps for the early driver. In this ad, a father tells his son about refueling the car and why he should always stop at a Bowser pump for "Pure and dry gasoline." With the crude measuring systems available, customers had to be reassured that they were getting what they paid for.

The Tokheim Dome Gasolene Outfit was one of the first gasoline pumps to see commercial use by the mid 1900s. Invented by John J. Tokheim in Thor, Iowa, it worked basically like a well pump for water. The operator would pump the handle in an up-and-down motion until gasoline filled the small 1 gallon glass cylinder, where it would be measured by markings on the glass and released through a valve-controlled spigot. *Gabriele Witzel*

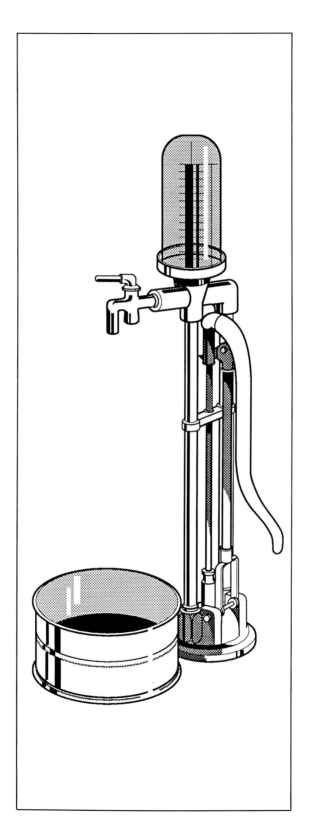

Sylvanus F. Bowser was a pioneer in the early field of gasoline pump development, designing a workable pump model by the year 1885. Planned originally as a device to pump coal oil or kerosene for use in lamps and stove heaters, his first prototype worked much like an ordinary well pump.

Constructed from a standard-size oil barrel with a wooden plunger mounted at its top and center, Bowser's pump worked on the vacuum principle to draw up fluid. A hand lever attached to the piston allowed a simple up-and-down motion to perpetuate the constant movement of liquid. At the top of the container, a spigot controlled the flow of kerosene into a tin receptacle for final measurement and sale. Overall, it was a rather crude device but distributed small amounts of coal oil to the public quite acceptably.

Bowser incorporated an organization under his name in Fort Wayne, Indiana, to manufacture this new invention and continued to produce a wide variety of petroleum-related equipment in the years that followed. Marketing hand-operated oil pumps, storage tanks and filtration systems to an ever-expanding petroleum industry, S. F. Bowser & Company ultimately proved successful with many of its petroleum industry ventures. As new machine tools and fixtures came into play, the company continued to make technical improvements on Bowser's original pump design. By 1905, an improved outdoor model suitable for pumping kerosene or gasoline was available for purchase.

This newly upgraded Bowser Self-measuring Gasoline Storage Pump consisted of a basic metal tank enclosed within a small wooden storage cabinet. Inside the weather-resistant housing, a pumping unit came complete with predetermined quantity stops, proper air venting for release of dangerous fumes and peripheral hardware required for operation. By moving a forced-suction plunger with a simple hand-stroke lever, one could quickly dispense gasoline. The Bowser pumps were easy to operate and made fuel more widely available than ever.

Many of Bowser's pump cabinets and others like it rapidly made their appearance in front of auto repair garages, general mercantile stores and other business establishments in urban and rural localities. The Bowser storage pumps became roadside fixtures on street corners throughout the country and made a lasting impression on gasoline purchasers. For years, fuel pumps were affectionately referred to as Bowsers, regardless of their particular manufacturer.

Tokheim's Triumph

Concurrent with the Bowser company's success, John J. Tokheim was experimenting with his own gasoline pumping unit in the small hamlet of Thor, Iowa. To speed up the pumping of kerosene at his retail hardware and well pump business, he set upon the task of locating a suitable pump. Because of particular specifications he had in mind, his choices for a suitable unit were limited. The type of pump Tokheim wanted didn't exist and a proper facsimile couldn't be readily located. So, he came up with a plan to design his own custom pump that operated according to his own guidelines.

After months of diligent work, the pump was finally completed and proved excellent for dispensing kerosene. Still not satisfied, Tokheim continued improvements and ultimately converted his first effort into a more workable unit for pumping gasoline.

By 1906, the Tokheim Dome Oil Pump outfit, as he called it, was ready to serve automobiles directly with gasoline. A combination visible and cylinder-measuring pump, it had a mechanical counter that was geared to the fluid-holding capacity of the cylinder and could be read for total gasoline volume pumped. Tokheim's dome pump was the first in the world to see widespread commercial use and became a leader in visible and cylinder-measuring pumps.

Built entirely from hollow tubing and cast-iron parts, Tokheim's pump featured extra-heavy-duty construction with all moving parts rustproofed. Sporting an all-brass cylinder and

valve, it boasted a self-measuring, water-separating glass dome. Up to one gallon of gasoline could be pumped into this inverted crucible and measured visually; a series of graduated markings painted on the glass denoted fractions of a standard gallon. If the dome was bypassed during pumping, gasoline could be delivered to an automobile's gas tank at the phenomenal rate of ten to twelve gallons per minute.

Complete with patented priming chamber to ensure quick discharge, the entire pump was set on a heavy metal stand that could be bolted down to a variety of surfaces. A little less than six feet in height, it weighed in at 135 pounds and was finished in red or black enamel with gold trim. A drip pan complete with grate and screen came furnished with the pump; the hose, nozzle and brass cutoff valve were available as options.

From the moment Tokheim's first hand pumps were put into commercial use, a new era had begun for the refueling of America's automobiles. The dangerous days of the funnel, measuring tin and chamois filter were fast coming to a close. Because new hand pumps could draw up fluid by creating a vacuum, gravity-fed tanks were eventually eliminated. The dangerous practice of storing highly flammable liquids in above-ground locations would soon be replaced by safer below-ground systems. Now, filling stations could be placed in more densely populated urban areas, since the only equipment taking up space would be the pump.

As the number of outlets supplying gasoline to motorists multiplied, the practicality and desirability of the automobile was acknowledged. A new level of gasoline availability was perceived by the public, leading to the eventual obsolescence of the hand-operated pumping devices pioneered by Bowser and Tokheim. Soon, pumping machines designed exclusively for dispensing the combustible fluid once regarded as a waste product by the oil industry would line every major street in America.

Wippel's Gas Station

Floyd Wippel's full-service gas station located in Ellensburg, Washington, used to be a major Main Street attraction. Automobiles came from all directions to stop in and purchase gasoline until one day the major routes were bypassed by a new freeway. Slowly, the once-busy thoroughfare outside his station gave way to local traffic.

No, never been in one of those 7–Elevens or new-fangled convenience stores where they sell gas and groceries. I buy all my gas right here at the station.

Floyd Wippel spends the hours waiting for customers inside a small stucco-covered building. A black and white television with coat hanger antenna sits in one corner of the room. An old radio sits on a shelf, its Bakelite case yellowed by time and the sun. In the corner, a small desk is piled high with notes and phone numbers scribbled on odd scraps of paper. A Victor hand-cranked cash register records the business transactions. In the center of the tiny room, an oil furnace burns to provide the heat. With turquoise glass electrical insulators attached to its legs, a wooden chair is one of the main pieces of furniture. On the wall above a phone hangs a faded sign: No long-distance calls.

As a customer pulls in, the ding-ding of the station bell sounds. Taking his time, Floyd slowly eases up from his creaking chair and heads out the door. In this part of Washington's Kittitas Valley, speed is unnecessary. The atmosphere is one of a small town and the local patrons who frequent the station still have the patience many city folks lost a long time ago. They still have time to chat and catch up on the latest news and gossip.

Floyd lifts the gas nozzle from the pump with a practiced motion honed over many years. Into the vehicle's tank it goes, providing combustible liquid just as it did for the Model A Ford and 1957 Chevrolet. Like time itself, the gallons swiftly click past as the mechanical counter records the numbers. For a moment, Floyd contemplates a past that could have been and the present that is—until a splurge of gas flowing over the filler neck jolts him from his thoughts. Awakened from his daydream, he continues to take care of the standard services a proper gas station provides, almost by

rote. After all these years, he still delights in providing the luxury of full service and making sure your car won't break down ten miles after pulling out of his station.

Floyd has been working his gas station for over forty-two years now. While others were busy being born, going through school or planning lifetimes, Wippel's gas station remained unchanged. It's as if the clock stopped for this one little parcel of ground on Highway 10 in downtown Ellensburg. Even the row of six vintage pumping units are still in operation. Their layers of old crackling paint mark the passing of years and long-forgotten dreams.

A faded maroon Chevy Powerglide stands parked beside the station just where it has always stood for the last four decades, still sporting the original tires and hubcaps. It was Floyd's first and only car. A Montana sticker graces a spot on one of the rear windows, perhaps collected from that one long trip, many years ago.

Back then, Highway 10 was a busy thoroughfare on the way to Yakima and the West. The gas stations in downtown Ellensburg prospered. To satisfy progress, a new freeway was constructed and the steady flow of tourists and traffic was permanently rerouted. A multitude of self-service stations and convenience marts were quickly constructed near the off ramps. Sprouting up like so many unchecked weeds, they grabbed a lion's share of the old business. Floyd's gas station would now serve only local customers and friends.

Slowly dipping a well-worn sponge into a bucket of soapy water, Floyd begins cleaning another windshield. With sweeping circular motions he moves his forearm, smearing dirt and water over the glass as the rhythm of his work blends with the flow of cars rushing past in the street. In Ellensburg, the wheels of time continue to pulsate and spin. Yet some things never change. They just can't. To do so would mean giving up cherished traditions and denying one's usefulness. A person who forges out a need for himself still exists, in his own mind and in the eyes of all humanity. A man is the maker of his own reality, his own destiny.

In Floyd's world, gas tanks are filled to their maximum capacity by a station attendant and the oil is checked without request. Air for tires is always free of charge and friendly service is rendered with a smile. The restrooms are always open, too.

For the countless motorists lucky enough to have experienced it, Wippel's full-service gas station has remained the same for over forty years just as it was the first day and hour it opened, business as usual. Sometimes, things never change.

Chapter 2

An Increasing Demand for Streetside Gas, 1908–1924

By 1908, advancements and improvements in motors, tires and all the other parts that made an automobile capable of locomotion were being hailed in every major publication favorable to the motorcar. Magazines like *Horseless Age* and *Motor World* reported on the latest engine designs offering more power over a wider range of rpm. *Cycle* and *Automobile Trade Journal* enlightened readers about new innovations that extended an engine's operational life, such as water cooling and force-feed oil pump lubrication, as well as the new magneto ignition systems that were soon to replace the impractical hand crank.

The public was introduced to the automobile's new comforts, too, as shock absorbers and independent springs eased the mechanical strain on automotive components—taking driving to a new level of enjoyment. Advertisements for "bonnets" and convertible tops became commonplace and offered the motorist protection from the elements. Who could fail to get excited when the steering wheel replaced the tiller control and acetylene headlamps ushered in the capability for night driving? Increasingly safe and reliable, the once-doubted automobile was fast becoming an all-weather machine for reliable transportation.

Mechanical durability was proven on a daily basis, and the practicality of owning a car instead of a horse was confirmed with every passing month. Every favorable automotive-related news story or fantastic publicity event presented by the nation's media was viewed with great interest by a car-crazy public. Once skeptical, people soon accepted the horseless vehicle as the way of the future, with many prominent citizens predicting the imminent replacement of the horse and buggy in both personal travel and commerce. Even the old-timer still in love with the simple ways of yesteryear began to grow accustomed to the idea of motorized transportation. The motorcar was finally gaining the great popularity its early inventors had hoped for as general acceptance grew.

Highly publicized "reliability tours" sponsored by millionaire automobile enthusiast Charles K. Glidden in early 1905 kindled that newfound excitement and contributed to the automobile's widespread demand. Extremely popular with horseless carriage aficionados, the first of these rambunctious tours covered an 870 mile road course starting in New York City. Navigated by eager contestants, gasoline-powered vehicles were required to negotiate a series of roads in the New England countryside and return to the city without breakdown. Elaborate trophies were presented to winners, and entry was open to all, providing ownership of the vehicle driven could be verified. Not surprisingly, the

Any business that wished to sell gasoline could do so in the early days of gasoline sales. All one had to do to start operations was secure a contract with a refiner, install a gas pump and underground tank, and put up the necessary signs to advertise a particular brand of fuel sold. Often, this led to a bad image for the oil companies, as buildings covered a wide variety of architectural styles and gave no hint to the quality and uniformity of a company's product. *Library of Congress*

Standing at salute next to a Tokheim Cut No. 850 Volumeter gasoline pump, this circa thirties Gulf station attendant is ready to pump the company's "good Gulf gasoline" into the tanks of motor vehicles. With military-style cap, jacket and matching jodhpur trousers, he conveys a willingness to help and the ability to offer the best service he can, with a friendly attitude. In the competitive arena of the thirties gasoline station, appearances were everything. *Chevron Corporation*

Streetside gasoline pumps like this Tokheim Curb Post Outfit No. 14 were some of the most modern pieces of equipment available in early 1910. Here, a White motorcar is refueled by use of a flexible hose and hand crank, stored inside a built-in pump cabinet. At night, the double electric signs atop the unit advertised gasoline for all who passed. *Tokheim Corporation*

tours quickly evolved into a showcase for every new model to roll out of the factory. Many tour contestants worked for major automotive manufacturers, and naturally they entered their company's latest offering.

The first of these tours took seven casualties, with twenty-seven of the thirty-four who entered completing the entire course. A heavy Pierce touring car was the first automobile to cross the finish line, carrying its five stylish passengers to jubilant victory. Spectators and entrants alike enjoyed themselves to the fullest in their mutual admiration of the automobile. The July 1905 issue of *Horseless Age* summed up the feelings of all those in attendance: The tour has proved that the automobile is now almost foolproof. It has proved that American cars are durable and efficient. It has shown the few who took part how delightful their short vacation may be, and it has strengthened our belief in the permanence of the motorcar.

An Automobile in Every Driveway

By creating a wealth of customers soon to join the ranks of new-car owners, the touted permanence of the motorcar would eventually ensure a bright future for all petroleum refining companies and their production of gasoline for profit. The clamor to obtain gasoline would increase proportionally with the unheard-of demand for the automobile, much to the surprise of the oil companies. Still, most motorized vehicles produced in this country were priced way out of reach of the working person's budget. Before gasoline pumps were to appear on every corner, automobile manufacturers had to recognize that the upper-class market catered to for so many years was becoming saturated with vehicles. An inexpensive and durable automobile had to be built.

Many companies chose to initiate the design and production of vehicles for the emerging middle-class market, and the contest to develop

Before factory-sealed oil cans were put into use, lubricating oil for automobiles was dispensed from a storage machine called a lubester and stored in quart-capacity glass bottles in a rack at the gas pump island. Like the Coke bottles returned to the grocery store for reuse, they eliminated the need to dispose of used containers, since they could be easily washed out or refilled for the next customer's purchase.

a reliable low-priced vehicle was fast underway. Despite the new agenda, dozens of car-building organizations stuck to their outmoded buggy designs and continued to sell them for a low price, including Ford's early competitor, Ransom E. Olds. Because of inherent construction flaws and mechanical weaknesses typical to their overall design, these surrey-styled vehicles proved to be highly unreliable. They rattled apart into useless assemblages of junk from the continual shaking of everyday use.

Simple in design with the most basic features, Ford's motor company based in Detroit introduced in 1906 what he considered to be his crowning achievement in life: the Model N Runabout. Fashioned in the image of the more expensive touring cars with front-mounted engine and the latest in technical achievements, it was a visionary offering. A highly reliable machine capable of a top speed of forty-five miles per hour, it had four cylinders that provided fifteen horsepower to drive its wheels. The Model N got great gas mileage, too: One gallon of fuel could quench its powerful engine for over twenty miles. The icing on the cake was a moderate price tag of $600, keeping the new motorcar well within reach of the many hopeful motorists that fantasized about owning a gasoline-powered vehicle.

Ford continued working on making the dream of motorcar ownership accessible to all and in doing so changed not only the way America traveled but the nature of society itself. By his introduction of the Model T in 1908, he moved closer than ever to his goal of creating an economical car for the masses. With eventual full implementation of the moving assembly line, he once and for all proved the Model T to be the car that put America on wheels.

At an initial selling price of only $850 for the standard touring version, over 19,000 Model Ts were quickly sold by the end of their first year. Manufacturing couldn't keep up with the demand. When the car was finally pulled from production some nineteen years later, its price had fallen to an all-time bargain of $290. By that time, one assembled automobile was rolling off the assembly line every twenty-four seconds, creating a total of 120 new cars every hour the factory worked. With Ford's initiation of a "living wage" for his assembly line workers, even his factory laborers could afford to purchase an automobile. To satisfy the increased demand for gas, additional refueling stations had to be constructed. Internal-combustion engines capable of burning copious amounts of gasoline throughout their useful life on the road would need refilling. Oils, greases, tires and the countless parts and services required to keep the new vehicles mobile called for new stations to be built. An army of service attendants had to be recruited to change spark plugs, fix linkages and pour oil into crankcases—and in their off moments pump gas to waiting customers.

Within only a few short years, an entire support industry with the automobile at its nucleus would have to materialize all along America's unfolding roadscape. High-volume production of low-priced cars for the great quantities of people who desired them had changed the nature of transportation. The floodgates at America's gasoline refineries were opened wide.

Here a Pump, There a Pump

The middle-class market embraced the automobile in America, and a new standard of mobility began to sweep the country. Soon regarded as the object of a basic right, like food and shelter, the automobile was considered a necessity for modern life. Only six years after the Model T's introduction, gasoline quickly replaced kerosene as the number one refined petroleum product in the country. By 1910, sales of motorized vehicles had risen more than 4,500 percent over the previous year, with the demand for gasoline rising at nearly the same clip. With the total number of cars in America's streets exceeding 350,000, oil companies had to develop many new locations to sell their gasoline—and fast.

Gasoline stations and the buildings that exclusively housed people and equipment for roadside refueling were still limited to the early bulk depots and the few garden-hose-type outlets that existed. The Automobile Gasoline Company had seen success in St. Louis with its station chain and Standard Oil in Seattle with its

outlet, but an organized system of retail gasoline outlets had yet to be formalized.

Standard Oil of California opened a small chain of thirty-four stations with standardized guidelines on the West Coast in 1914. A few other drive-in establishments with pumps existed, but they were the exception, as most refueling locations remained a hodgepodge of businesses originated for other purposes. Limited in number, structures dedicated to the refueling of automobiles were still in the minority. New methods had to be developed to distribute gasoline to the myriad new motorists in search of a full gas tank.

To maximize quick profit return and realize low initial expenditures, the gasoline-producing oil companies initiated a crash campaign to secure existing businesses as new outlets to sell their gasoline to the public. With the new Burton cracking processes introduced in 1913 to better process gasoline, larger quantities of fuel could now be refined from the same amount of petroleum. Soon, this glut of gasoline could be purchased virtually anywhere along urban taxpayer strips, city streets or country roadsides. Naturally, businesses closely related to the field of travel took to this campaign of distribution without thinking twice. Almost overnight, bicycle shops, automotive dealers, car garages and carriage

Shell Oil Company's first Seattle depot, at Westlake Avenue and Highland Drive, opened during the fall of 1912. Horsedrawn tank wagons still carried gasoline to customers. At the time this 1913 photo was taken, D. G. Fisher— for over twenty years Shell's division manager for the Northwest—was the company's sole salesperson. Today, Shell's Seattle office building occupies the site. *Shell Oil Company*

Jack Collier and the stone station his father constructed by hand decades ago. Surviving all these years, it still looked as good in 1989 as the day it was completed.

The Stone Gas Station

When I was five years old I started putting water in the cars, when I turned nine I started serving the cars like my dad did. I was already big enough to pump gas by then.

Stones—thousands of them! That's what Jack Collier's unique service station on Rainier Avenue, Seattle, is made of. Void of any rare compounds or flecks of precious gold in their oblong structure, they aren't anything special. Just well-worn river rocks easily cradled in the palm of the hand, they are composed of the simple elements in nature: carbon, hydrogen, oxygen—maybe some iron. Jack's dad could have used brick back in 1926 when he first started constructing the building, but that would have been too easy. Rounded stones were much more beautiful and appealed to his aesthetics as a mason. Compressed by the natural forces of the earth, they could withstand the ultimate test of time and were perfectly suited for his monumental labor of love.

Jack fondly remembers those crazy days when his father first opened his gas business. American cars were the rule, and names like Packard and Ford dominated the boulevard. Cars were much easier to service, and simple tasks like the oil and lube job were part of the station attendant's routine. Getting someone to fix a flat wasn't the chore it is today, as mechanics gladly helped with even the smallest of problems. When hoods were opened, simple engines were revealed, not the jumble

30

of components crammed inside today's "advanced" vehicles. The automobile was vastly different in those innocent days, and the business of running a gas station uncomplicated.

Tall visible-register gasoline pumps were the vogue, indicative of the current technology. Pumped by hand or electric motor, a volatile mixture of Ethyl would slowly fill a glass cylinder, then quickly drain into the vehicle's gas tank. Fuel was completely "visible," and the customer could see that some kind of liquid was flowing into the car. Some companies even colored their gas to promote sales, as Gilmore Oil Company did with its Blu-Green brand. Slogans like Roar with Gilmore and The new and better Texaco gasoline barraged the motoring consumer. Madison Avenue was just learning how to sell the roadway to the nation.

The American work ethic thrived at Collier's Service Station. Living and breathing the business, the entire family helped run the station. Jack was only five years old when he was initiated into the fold by helping his father put water into automobile radiators. When he turned nine, he graduated to helping cars at the pumps. Everyone took equal turns performing their fair share of the work, with one of them always excluded from finishing dinner. But that wasn't a problem for Jack's mother; servicing cars provided her with a great deal of personal satisfaction. Dressed in a classic white uniform and apron, she loved taking care of the customers and worked the station well into her golden years.

For a good portion of his life, Jack served the roadway, fueling the freedom of a society in love with the automobile and road travel. Among the last of the vanishing breed known to provide quality and service, he closed the business forever in 1963. The man who was once a boy barely strong enough to carry a can of water to an overheated car became the final one in his family to operate the station and pump gasoline.

But even after Jack and the taillights of his motor home have disappeared over the horizon, the station and its curious stones will continue to endure. If torn apart to make way for a new shopping center, their long journey from creation and back will start anew. Dismantled, they will become a pile of rocks again. If they aren't reused in another structure, they will inevitably be taken to a landfill and dumped. Resting there for half an eternity, their basic elements will be unaffected until the day they become part of a new legacy.

Jack's unique stone station looked quite different in 1947. Back then, Jack's father sold the Clipper brand of gasoline from the visible-register gas pumps. Cars were of a different variety too, and it wasn't unusual to see a 1935 Studebaker Dictator like the one parked near the side of the station pull up for gas or service. Jack Collier

Almost completely rusted out, the Bowser-brand pumps that once serviced the roadway at Jack's stone station stood dormant and unused in 1989, out on the service island. Closed down since the sixties, they were now only broken reminders of the traffic that used to stop in to get tanks refilled.

Gilbert & Barker Company introduced its T–1 nonregistering hand pump early in 1910. The unit operated with a simple up-and-down motion, much like a tire pump. A flexible hose attached to the side of it allowed the operator to refill the gas tank of a vehicle with relative ease, providing he or she knew when to stop pumping. In relation to the tiller-steered vehicle in the background, the mechanical complexity of these early pump devices was adequate. *Gilbarco Inc.*

shops all had gasoline pumps installed in front of their establishments. Hardware stores, feed companies, livery stables and general retailers joined the rush, too.

Virtually any business owner who wished to sell gasoline could have a pump and storage tank installed outside his or her shop and advertise gasoline for sale. Because thousands of these new income-generating outlets could be easily obtained by the oil giants in a matter of months, the need to secure new real estate space was bypassed. Profits from the sale of gasoline could be realized in a short time, as oil distributors were only required to install pumps, deliver the gas and collect their huge share of the profits. Individual shop owners would do all the sales work and collect the generous revenues to come.

Since current demand outstripped all supply, the merchants didn't mind doing their part to sell gasoline to the steady stream of eager motorists that would soon pass by their new curbside installations. Within a short time, the unmistakable gasoline pump could be spied from almost any streetside vantage point, the automobile almost always nearby.

Gas Pumps That Made It Happen

The drum-and-measure method was far too impractical and dangerous for the growing number of businesses that wished to supply fuel for the motorist. Safe devices that delivered gaso-

line with expediency and user convenience became a basic necessity for every streetside fuel vendor. Workable by almost any operator with varying skill level, these new gasoline pump designs had to be simple to install and easily repaired on-site. For large quantities of motor fuel to be sold, the dispensing of gasoline had to be freed from the burdens of the early bulk operations.

Without advances in gasoline pump technology developed by a number of manufacturers, the unprecedented haste employed by major oil companies to secure gasoline dealers wouldn't have been possible. The Gilbert & Barker Company (Gilbarco) was one of the first to introduce a practical pumping unit with the development of the T–8 one-gallon hand pump in 1912. Utilizing quantity stops and an all-metal housing to hide internal gearing and mechanical components, it had an overall demeanor of uniformity and permanence. A quick-discharge piston could deliver fluid at a rate of fifteen gallons per minute, with a simple dial indicator reading the amount of gas pumped. White lettering across the pump's front access door spelled out Filtered Gasoline, and an etched glass globe supported atop the pump by an extrusion repeated the simple description.

Magazine advertisements trumpeting the Tokheim Oil Tank & Pump Company's Curb Post Outfit No. 14 touted many built-in promotional features that made it worth more than its selling price. With a post of solid cast iron and a commanding stature of over eight feet, it sported double electric signs that were claimed to attract the attention and admiration of all who passed—day or night. Facilitated by advanced internal illumination, perforated metal inserts displayed the availability of new brands of gas or posted the station name and owner. "Simple and as substantially built as human hands could make them," said Tokheim copywriters, who lauded the new pumps as the most modern type of gasoline dispensing equipment available. For the motorist, that would mean clean, filtered and accurately measured gasoline.

As more of these modern pump units appeared on the market, gasoline storage went permanently underground, simplifying the

ness within the state were of the curb-site variety, the controversial ruling spelled disaster.

Standard Oil Company of New York (Socony) sold gasoline through hundreds of these streetside pumps and was forced to take drastic steps in order to maintain its share of sales. The oil giant wasted no time in responding by hastily forming its own internal real estate department. Almost overnight, new station sites and available business property in the areas affected by the ban were purchased. Suddenly, oil companies had to invest much more of their own capital to obtain sales locations in order to operate their gas pumps within legal boundaries.

Outmoded by time, the swelling number of vehicles and the changing structure of America's roadways, the curbside gasoline pump had eventually seen the last of its days as a primary source for gasoline dispensing. In the future, it would survive only in conjunction with the rural general store or streetside business located within an area of low traffic congestion. Soon, most public outlets selling gasoline would be housed in a single structure situated on a separate lot, with multiple pumps serving numerous vehicles at the same time. The evolution of the filling station and its transformation into an autonomous roadside business had become a necessity.

Chapter 3

The Gas Station Boom Years, 1925-1932

The first businesses to exclusively sell gasoline by the roadside were usually housed in poorly constructed shacks or makeshift sheds. Independent operators interested only in making a fast buck signed a contract with an oil company one day, installed a few gasoline pumps the next, threw up a couple of signs and were in business. Adding to the already unwanted visual clutter created by the countless other urban businesses involved in the commercial sale of bulk commodities, the ramshackle filling station could easily be installed on any vacant lot or busy street where vehicles passed—creating an overnight eyesore.

Usually made up of whatever cheap construction materials were readily available, these early gas shanties lacked charm or visual appeal. Often, tarpaper covered a shaky frame of scrap wood or metal sheeting enclosed an unplanned assembly of nailed-together braces. Features such as canopies or roof overhangs for shelter from the elements were nonexistent and universally regarded as unnecessary. Since most vehicles of the day were not fully enclosed, these stations were normally used only in fair weather.

When it rained, automobiles sloshed through muddy driveways that mirrored the unimproved dirt roadbeds already a standard to reach these unimposing structures. In some rare instances, when finances allowed, marginal improvement resulted with the addition of gravel. But for the most part, the uncomplicated gasoline businesses of the flapper era were unappealing. Uncloaked on the roadside with their unmaintained gasoline pumps, motor oils, greases and other grimy equipment necessary for motorized vehicles, the gasoline buildings made their utilitarian status all too evident for the cars that drove by.

Little Gas Shacks

Even with the approximately 15,000 gasoline stations operating in the United States in 1920, most building designs still took rudimentary forms. Why construct an expensive hut to house a station attendant? The purchase of gasoline pumps and the installation of underground fuel tanks were enough of an expense for the early station proprietors. A customized structure intended solely for the pumping of fuel into an empty gas tank seemed frivolous. Eventually, however, the unprofessional features of these unregulated gasoline businesses became a prime source of concern to the homeowner and passing motorist. Increasingly educated about motoring, the public grew leery of shoddy operators and the frequently inferior quality of fuel and equipment that matched the rundown gas shack's outward appearance.

Because crude gas stations gave the entire industry a bad name, the major oil companies took notice and initiated the construction of

CONTAINS LEAD

(TETRAETHYL) AND IS TO BE USED AS MOTOR FUEL ONLY, NOT FOR CLEANING OR ANY OTHER USE. AVOID SPILLING.

One of many free items once passed out by yesterday's service stations, this Flying A brand gasoline station advertising button is now a much-sought-after collectible.

By 1910, regular gasoline establishments like this Central Oil gas station in Flint, Michigan, appeared all over the United States. Constructed in simple shedlike styles of corrugated metal sheeting and other materials and easily installed on any vacant lot or busy street where vehicles passed, the ramshackle filling station was an overnight eyesore. *American Petroleum Institute*

more unified buildings. They scrambled to make changes, and soon the level of customer service and quality of products found at a gas station in Hoboken, New Jersey, would be the same as that at an exact duplicate located in El Cajon, California.

Shell Oil Company discovered the selling advantages of a central design theme early in the game of gasoline retailing with its operation of standardized company stations throughout the West Coast. Of the 1,841 retail outlets supplied with its gasoline, more than 200 were built with common design aspects. Featuring the same stylized graphics, color schemes, pump equipment, uniforms and customer station policies, the company's unified station models accounted for well over forty percent of 1922 gasoline sales in their marketing domain.

Fun in the Linear Slum

The general public began to view the unchecked proliferation of the gasoline station with mixed emotions. On one hand, vehicle owners welcomed the idea that gasoline could now be obtained virtually anywhere without fear of running out. But, they also worried about the ever-increasing number of unsightly buildings

popping up wherever the automobile roamed. Zoning ordinances had only recently been instituted for curbside pumps. Regulations governing the rapid expansion of entire pumping stations wherever proprietors wished to construct them were yet to be written.

Lacking any attractive visual attributes, many of these tumbledown filling stations infiltrated urban business districts and residential areas. Discordant structures with greasy surroundings serving a noisy procession of smoking and honking vehicles, these refueling eyesores were largely unwanted in many populated areas. Extra traffic generated by the transient nature of their business threatened to clutter once peaceful streets where "little Johnny" played and horses clip-clopped their way across town.

In rural areas, the public's growing sentiment against the burgeoning gasoline station and its image was magnified by the practice of businesses, including gasoline stations, placing "snipe" signs hawking various brands of gasoline, tobacco, groceries, welding or other unrelated goods by the roadside. These hand-painted billboards covered every inch of space at roadside stops and contributed heavily to the roadside blight. Mile by mile, a linear slum was slowly forming along many of America's most scenic routes.

In the opinion of prominent civic leaders and roadside reformers, these unorganized collages installed plainly for advertising purposes contributed to the visual strangulation of the roadscape's beauty. Most motorists who drove to the country expressly seeking nature—and to get away from the hustle of the city—weren't impressed by poor rural businesses that felt it was their right to benefit from the new traffic passing by. Until some sort of compromise could be reached, the automobilist's prerogative to view the countryside in an untainted state would continue to be violated by the wants of commerce, the sale of goods and services taking precedence over bucolic views.

Beautification of the Roadside

Supporters of the City Beautiful movement were growing increasingly uneasy about the

Claiming to be the first "drive-in" filling station in the United States, this structure built by Standard Oil Company in 1912 at Oak and Young streets in Columbus, Ohio, offered the motorist new convenience. Now, the motorcar operator could drive through one end of the building, get refueled and drive out the other. *Standard Oil Company of Ohio*

In response to the pleas of the City Beautiful movement, the Atlantic Refining Company of Pennsylvania erected some of the first stations inspired by the ancient structures of classical Greece. The magnificent new buildings were major works of architecture. This station was located in Pennsylvania. *American Petroleum Institute*

Eventually, Jerry Chinn hopes to restore the Keeler's Korner gas station and grocery store and make it into a static roadside diorama depicting the small-town gas station of the late twenties. Jerry is an avid collector of antiques and service station memorabilia and has turned his hobby into a profession. Now operating a professional set and prop business in Seattle, he comes well suited for the task of restoring the Korner to its former glory.

Its eye gouged out, one of two Flying Red Horse Pegasus signs mounted atop the canopy at Keeler's Korner stands a tireless vigil, waiting for today's "service station" to revert back to the old ways of service and quality.

Keeler's Korner

My grandparents owned a gas station and grocery in Haldane, Illinois. I'd work for a dollar a day pumping gas, slicing meat and stocking shelves . . . and had a blast doing it!

When Keeler's Korner first opened in 1927, transportation technology was still in its infancy. Infatuated with the magic of the motorcar, eager drivers dreamed up every excuse they could think of to hit the road. Traveling over the highways and byways of rural America was the real fun back then, and scores of automobile enthusiasts delighted in taking the smallest of journeys. Motorized jalopies raced down highways at speeds of up to thirty miles per hour as neighbors sat on their front porches lamenting the demise of the horse-drawn carriage. An awareness for the simple pleasures in life prevailed, and time to revel in the moment was more appreciated. The "ride" was more important than the destination.

More than fifty years have passed since those innocent days, and the once-relaxed stretch of Highway 99 that eased past Keeler's Korner has undergone some unthinkable changes. Now one of the most dangerous strips of traffic congestion in Washington State, it serves the utilitarian purpose of alternate traffic route. Bypassing the daily gridlock of Seattle's impassable freeways, nameless faces scramble across its level asphalt to cheap motels, used-car lots and discount appliance stores. Tightly locked and safety-belted into their vehicles, impatient commuters anonymously traverse its hectic path on their way to work. Slowing only briefly to grab a greasy breakfast sandwich or a cup of java at the 7-Eleven, they move like the lemming with single-minded purpose. In the rush of mindless frenzy, no time is left to savor the moment.

Somehow, the quaint green and white building Carl Keeler built during the Roaring Twenties to house a gas station and general store has survived the invasion. Unaffected by progress and the progressive rethinking of Lynnwood's urban landscape, its friendly aura still conjures up feelings of security for those who take the time to look. Tucked away between towering evergreens, it still looks much as it did fifty-five years ago. With a simple cottage style, it strikes a harsh contrast to the discordant appearance of today's exaggerated modern. In juxtaposition to the halogen glare of Seattle's impersonal shopping malls, it's not what the motorist would expect to see on the Twentieth-Century roadside.

Looking for available real estate, Jerry Chinn spied the unique structure back in the sixties and was so taken by the site that he decided to open his antique shop there. His business became successful—enabling him to later purchase the Korner and place it on the historic register. Perfectly suited for the job of restoring the building with his creative skills in art direction and set design, he moved into the upstairs portion and made it his home. Utilizing his talents, he began the slow process of transforming the decaying structure into his final vision of a static museum. Turning back the clock will take some effort, but he is determined to rebuild this roadside slice of life from another era and recreate it as an authentic diorama of the past.

The restored station won't be anything new for Jerry. He grew up in that kind of atmosphere, his affinity for the charm of the classic service station being deeply rooted in his childhood. Many a long summer's afternoon was spent at his grandparent's service station in Haldane, Illinois, playing and pumping gas. Helping his grandfather stock shelves and his grandmother slice meat, he earned the lucrative wages of a dollar a day. To him, it was not a real job but a personal, life-size playground where a starry-eyed boy could play out his childhood fantasies.

Like most people, Jerry grew up and lost hold of his dream and the simple satisfaction that it brought him in his youth. Luckily, it stayed alive over the passage of years in his thoughts and memories, to be lovingly recreated with the resurrection of Keeler's Korner. With the station's completion, he hopes to deliver that personal fantasy to everyone else who dares to dream of how things used to be along America's roadways.

As early as 1915, Shell Oil Company of California utilized a prefabricated metal design manufactured by a number of companies like the Michelle & Pfeffer Iron Works of San Francisco for its standard station design. With flat roof, a one-post canopy, electric illumination and modern gasoline pumps, it projected a clean and efficient image to the motorist passing by. *Shell Oil Company*

unappealing genre of commercial structures appearing on the roadside and were particularly disturbed about gasoline stations. The architectural directions being taken by independent operators and some oil companies were less than desirable to the movement's supporters. In their opinion, the undignified filling station building was threatening to become a permanent blot upon the landscape.

First introduced at the Chicago Columbian Exposition of 1893 as a philosophy for organized civic development with high regard to visual aesthetics, the ideals of the City Beautiful movement espoused virtues of planned construction within certain architectural guidelines. At the exposition, architects schooled in Europe revealed a new concept for urban arrangement by constructing white beaux-arts palaces influenced by

ancient Rome and the great Renaissance cities. Their great White City constructed for public view followed the parameters of classical design to the letter.

Proponents of the movement wanted to inject some of these stylings into the everyday life of motorists and dreamed of constructing a network of parklike corridors for automobile travel, complete with dramatic scenery and roadside structures in the class of respectable monuments. To them, majestic fountains, paved esplanades, open plazas and natural landscaping were more important than the blatant commercialism threatening to sully America's skyline.

Unable to silence the cries for reform, a few progressive oil conglomerates soon caved in to pressure from the pleas of the City Beautiful

supporters. The Atlantic Refining Company (Arco) of Pennsylvania upscaled its normal agenda for station design and erected some of the first of the magnificent new stations. A scaled-down version of the monument to Lysicrates in Athens, Greece, one of its revolutionary new gas stations, was surrounded by an Ionic colonnade inspired by the Erechtheum where Pallas Athene waged war with Poseidon. Like the local bank or city hall in any large town, it was intended to command an instant level of civic pride with its monumental stature and neoclassical detailing. The *American City* magazine, a major supporter of the City Beautiful movement, reported the opening of this artistic structure with gushing enthusiasm in August 1922:

"The building is constructed of white terracotta, and its perfect proportions will linger long in the memory. This charming reproduction of one of the finest bits of Greek architecture extant forms a striking contrast to the great majority of buildings erected for the purpose of supplying the wants of modern charioteers."

For entrepreneurs on a budget, prefabricated units with pressed-metal pilasters embodying the same classical motifs of the City Beautiful movement could be delivered and assembled in a matter of days. To supply the growing demand, manufacturers like the Arthur B. Sheppard Company, Michelle & Pfeffer Iron Works, and later California Cornice and Steel Supply offered a variety of models to the gas industry. Made entirely of metal components, they were easily bolted together at the building site and had the ability to be moved quickly when a station location proved unprofitable. For the economical price of $2,200, one could purchase a future gas station on Monday, have it

Complete with cobblestone drive and eight drive-up gasoline pumps disguised in small cabinets, this Atlantic Refining Company station was only one of the many artistic stations constructed in response to the criticisms of the City Beautiful movement and the denigration of the tumble-down filling station proliferating along America's roadways. *American Petroleum Institute*

45

Tokheim Oil Tank & Pump Company product bulletin. Cut No. 290 Hi-way Hand-operated Five-Gallon Capacity Visible Gasoline Dispenser. Circa 1923. *Tokheim Corporation*

Next page
Gulf Oil Company's first drive-in gasoline service station opened in Pittsburgh at the corner of Baum Boulevard and St. Clair Street in 1913. The brainchild of W. V. Hartmann, general sales manager, the new station sold an average of 1,800 gallons per day by the following spring. Inspired by a letter written to the company inquiring where one could find that "good Gulf gasoline," the company utilized the catchphrase in station advertising and promotion of its products. *Chevron Corporation*

QUALITY TOKHEIM
COMPLETE FILLING STATION AND BULK STORAGE EQUIPMENT
FACTORY STORAGE AND DISTRIBUTING SYSTEMS

Bulletin No. 210   Cut 290

Cut No. 290
Hi-way Hand-Operated
Five-Gallon Capacity
Visible
Gasoline Dispenser

The symmetrical and attractive design makes this an ideal pump for use in Filling Stations or at the Curb.

In its construction many unique and distinctive features have been incorporated, thus insuring the widest possible range of service.

PREDOMINANT FEATURES:

Flood-type electric illumination of the entire pump.

Three gallonage indicators, prominently located on the outside of the glass measuring cylinder.

Two hose discharge connections—one at the front, the other at the side of pump.

Overhead fill located within the glass cylinder.

Speedy, horizontal, double-acting plunger pump.

Numerous interlocking features—affording equal protection to both dealer and customer.

Exclusive **TOKHEIM** design and construction throughout.

delivered that afternoon and be ready for the first customer to drive through the Ionic columns to get gas on Thursday.

Dignified Designs and Signs

Sponsored by Mrs. John D. Rockefeller, Jr., in conjunction with the Adolph Goebel Company (a New York hot dog manufacturer), the American Civic Association and the Art Center of New York, roadside reformers endeavored to make further gains in the beautification of the American roadscape in 1927. With hopes to foster a heightened awareness for roadside aesthetics throughout the states, a series of national design contests offered prizes for the most visually appealing roadside stands and gasoline stations already existing. At the same time, new building designs that didn't offend the casual motorist's senses were requested for entry. Based on overall visual appeal and functionality, the originator of these new plans would receive an award.

That same year, the Union Oil Company of California (Unocal) launched a nationwide search for a "dignified filling station" design. More than 100 entries were received by the company, covering a surprisingly wide variety of

treatments. A highly detailed octagonal pavilion with white stucco walls captured first prize and in combination with the second-place entry influenced the design of a new line of stations for Union Oil Company's new southwest territory. Their roofs covered in Spanish tile and bright walls gleaming in white stucco, small octagonal kiosks with complementing pump islands soon appeared throughout Union's arid territories.

Standard Oil of California continued in the tradition of upgrading roadside scenery and company image by deciding to remove 1,200 immense circular billboards advertising its Red Crown gasoline in 1924. Scattered throughout the western United States, these fifteen foot diameter monstrosities with their bright red lettering and graphics branded an indelible image on the landscape. Yet, down they came as Standard's new policy of voluntary removal improved the view from behind the steering wheel.

Continuing efforts for beautification brought about Standard's Sign-ic or scenic contest in 1929. Entrants were called upon to send in essays presenting new solutions for ending the widespread installation of "objectionable advertising signs along the highway" as well as to give their opinions on what should be done about the growing problem. With witty slogans such as Why Sign Away Beauty? and Landmarks—Not Trademarks, a sampling of photographs submitted by contestants illustrated just how easily scenic beauty could be obscured by commercial signs. When it came to defacing nature, Standard learned that it could be held accountable for its actions and had to keep the aesthetic interests of the public in mind.

No Place Like Home

Growing increasingly aware that station image conveyed a host of messages to the gasoline-purchasing public, the Pure Oil Company decided to revitalize its station structures. A newly formed merger absorbing smaller companies resulted in a station roster consisting of grossly mismatched styles of architecture—some marginally acceptable, many quite unappealing. President Henry M. Dawes was seeking a new "shirtfront" for the company and desired

Petersen's English-cottage-style station provided a new image for Pure Oil Company's gasoline stations. Offering up hearth and home, it promised an atmosphere greatly missed by the traveler. *Keith A. Sculle Collection*

a distinctively new building style that could be readily associated with the Pure gasoline brand for all its combined outlets.

Self-taught architect Carl August "C. A." Petersen went to work on the task in the mid-twenties a short while after Dawes offered him an increase in salary to join Pure's team. Upset that his house ideas were rejected by former employer Gulf Oil Company, Petersen was eager to design a unique station structure to unify the ragtag image of Pure. By working diligently at home to avoid any unwanted suggestions, he soon had a distinctive, easy-to-build

and inexpensive English-cottage-style station completed on the drawing board.

Featuring a high-pitch gable roof made up of blue tiles, his cottage motif called for all exterior woodwork in white, with window shutters and moldings to match the roof. Two tall chimneys would be situated at both ends of the structure, with blue chimney pots and red-faced brick trimming the tops. To signify the Pure affiliation, a metal cutout of the letter *P* in elongated Old English lettering was to be affixed to the exterior of each flue. A variety of models were drafted, the simplest housing only an office and a toilet and more elaborate elevations containing dual greasing bays housed under their own angular roofs.

Dawes liked the completed drawings so much that after viewing them he presented Petersen with a bonus check for $750—right out of his own pocket. His enthusiasm was well-founded, for the designs proved economical to build and could be constructed from a number of basic materials. More important, the motoring public liked the way the stations looked and eventually came to view the English cottage style as being synonymous with Pure's quality petroleum products. Whether erected on a quiet residential street or a busy urban thoroughfare, the structures always fit in well on the roadside. With the success of the Pure Oil Company and the acceptance of the C. A. Petersen station designs, the house was firmly established as a viable architectural form for the American gasoline station structure.

From the vantage point of the motorist wheeling past, the pleasant trappings of the roadside house conjured up welcome feelings of friendliness and offered the atmosphere so greatly missed by the traveler when venturing forth on the open road. The mere sight of a white-shuttered window spilled forth memories of Mom and those delicious home-baked pies cooling on the sill. A house meant quiet evenings by the fireside with one's favorite dog or the whole family huddled around the radio listening in on the exploits of Fibber McGee and Molly. It was a safe, warm and happy place for many and a common association that would be exploited to maximum potential by hundreds of roadside

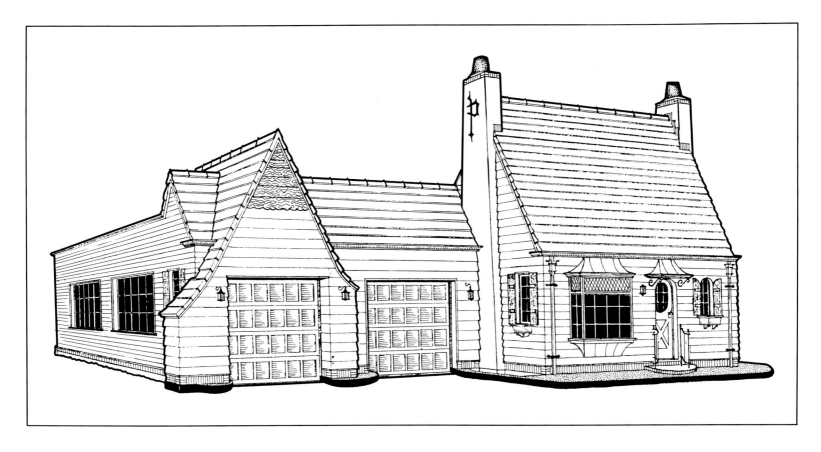

eaties, motels and gasoline stations that were constructed in its image.

The house quickly developed into the most popular form of architecture for gasoline sales and was readily accepted for installation in the midst of most suburban communities. Soon, residential building sites and prime corner lots were being purchased by many of the large oil concerns in the hopes of constructing new domestic stations. Because the house fit in so well and in some cases was regarded as an "architectural asset," the move toward new restrictive ordinances and construction bans was eased. As widespread acceptance of the house grew, focus was taken off the oil companies and their consumptive real estate acquisitions.

Gasoline Becomes Visible

The blind gasoline pumps that first appeared streetside at the earliest gasoline stations rapidly became outmoded and inefficient. Suspicious motorists felt isolated from the product they were purchasing and were never really confident of its quality and purity. The public wanted to know what was flowing into the tanks of their prized possessions and to see what it looked like, too.

Some of the first devices that made this possible were modification kits for use on existing pump products such as the 1912 Gilbert & Barker T-8 curbside gasoline pump. With a dial indicator standard on the original model, it was easily retrofitted to utilize a five-gallon glass cylinder and could be upgraded with a new globe attachment advertising "visible gasoline." A proprietor already in possession of the basic pump could quickly modify the unit to reflect the new visible style with a minimal cash investment and only minor installation work.

Within a short time, all new gasoline pumps were constructed in the visible-register design, making upgrading unnecessary. Manufacturers like Guaranteed Liquid Measure Company, Fry, Wayne Oil Tank & Pump Company and S. F.

Designed by C. A. Petersen, the Pure house came in a variety of styles. The service bays that soon became a necessity to lubricate and repair vehicles could easily be integrated into the design to look like any suburban garages. *Jerry Keyser Collection*

Bowser & Company introduced a number of visible pumps to the market and began to advertise their superior features in leading industry journals.

Though the pumps all appeared to be slightly different, a basic mode of operation was common to almost every model. From an underground storage tank, fuel was pumped by means of a rotary hand crank and filled a clear glass crucible. Two discharge levers controlled the liquid: one allowed gasoline to flow from the cylinder into an automobile; the other operated a drain-back valve connected to the storage tank buried below. When one engaged, the other locked in place, causing gasoline released in either direction to be limited to that movement. When the desired volume of gasoline was reached in the cylinder above, the proper switch was activated, causing gasoline to flow through a hose into the vehicle's gas tank.

Some units such as the Tokheim Cut No. 290 Hi-way Hand-operated pump offered a two-way horizontal plunger design that allowed for faster pumping by means of quick forward movements of a long lever. With only fourteen strokes, an operator could fill the glass cylinder to capacity within ten to twelve seconds. Located in the suction line directly beneath the pump, an internal filter removed all foreign matter and water as the gasoline was drawn through.

The round glass cylinder that gave the pumping device its name was securely mounted high atop a cylindrical support base made of heavy metal or cast iron. Situated alongside the cylinder wall, graduated markers descending in numerical order from the top of the cylinder indicated the total number of gallons present. Whether fashioned from metal or etched into the glass, these gallon markers registered the amount of gasoline pumped from the ground and into the glass receptacle before sale.

Unfortunately, the visible-register gas pump was still vulnerable to error and cheating, since the gallon markers could easily be misaligned. The demarcations could also be difficult to read by customers with poor eyesight, since the height of the pump was often considerable. Compounding the problem, the contents of the visible crucible often expanded when the sun's

On the backcountry roads, the local general store often erected a gas pump to offer service. The Pearce General Store, off old 666 in southwest Arizona, has survived the ravages of time and still operates in the nineties. Once an old mining town, Pearce has seen its share of wild times.

With automobiles lined up in the street, Phillips Petroleum Company's first service station in Wichita, Kansas, opened for business November 19, 1927. It marked the company's jump from being a small oil and gas producer. *Courtesy Phillips Petroleum Company*

rays heated the glass jar, causing the fuel to push through an overflow valve and run back into the underground storage tank. To get the most gasoline for the money during the summer, purchases had to be planned for the evening or other cool periods of the day. Though reassuring to customers desiring to see their gasoline, the visible-register gasoline pump wasn't always as accurate as motorists thought it was.

Cylinder capacity was initially limited to five gallons, with some pump manufacturers intro-

ducing larger ten-gallon units by the early twenties. Added conveniences such as electrically operated floodlamps were available for installation to illuminate both the pump and the cylinder area for night business. For more protection, a rigid net of expanded steel mesh often surrounded the glass beaker, replaced by thin metal tubes spaced at close intervals on later versions. Fitted with a curved brass nozzle without its own shutoff valve, a metal-lined hose ten feet in length attached to the base of the cylinder. A pump handle equipped with an integral trigger for controlling fluid flow was still on the drawing board.

Majestic Monoliths

As refueling stations became more refined in their design and construction, so did the gasoline pumps that made business such a success. New models soon featured ornate trim castings and polished brass or chrome fittings. Gleaming cylinder bars surrounded by four curved external tubings protected the top container of many visible pumps such as the Fry 117. With wide base, long tapered stalk and bulging glass cylinder, pump designs mirrored the fashion of the day—mimicking the exaggerated female form of the era. Easily stealing a driver's attention from the roadside, these graceful Mae West pumps were often finished in extravagant colors, topped with conspicuous glass globes illuminated from within.

The combination of dazzling metals and flowing design made the visible-register pumps as enjoyable to look at as they were to operate. With a grace and style foreign to today's pump designs, they delivered gasoline to the American automobile in a class by themselves. More than eight feet in height, they towered over the roadside with an opulent grandeur unmatched by any gasoline pump of the present day, commanding attention from all directions. When maintained properly by station personnel, the visible-register gasoline pump was a sight to behold.

Yet, pump manufacturers felt that more visually appealing designs were needed to help bolster the cause of overall station appearance and company image. With the influence of the City Beautiful movement effecting changes in architecture, new pumps were in demand by many oil companies wishing to complement the new stations. In light of this requirement, Wayne introduced the Cut No. 490 series of visible-register gasoline pump. Influenced by the Ionic columns of ancient Greece, designers fashioned fluted cast-iron cylinders typical of archaic architectural pedestals. With decorative pump details influenced by the Temple of Wingless Victory in ancient Athens cradling the glass cylinder, they

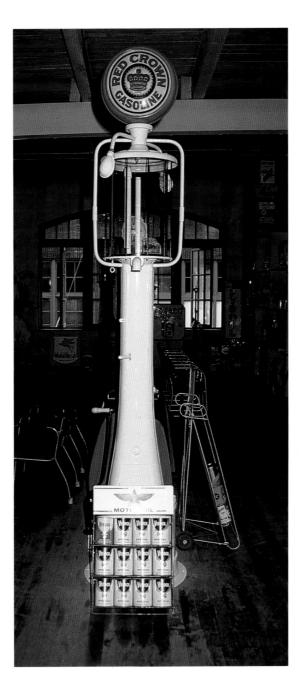

Mae West visible-register gasoline pump on display at the General Petroleum Museum

lent an immediate aura of dignity to any station installation. Considered by many to be the most beautiful gasoline pumps ever manufactured, the units making up the new Wayne product line were at the height of their form as ornate mechanical devices before the radical influences of the coming age of machine aesthetics.

53

National gasoline coupon books from the Octagon Service Station chain were often used during the thirties as a means to bring in new customers. By paying in advance for an entire booklet of coupons, the motorist could realize a nice savings on fuel purchases. Of course, if the booklet was lost, it would be just the same as losing money. *Octagon Service Station*

QUALITY
TOKHEIM

COMPLETE FILLING STATION AND BULK STORAGE EQUIPMENT
FACTORY STORAGE AND DISTRIBUTING SYSTEMS

Bulletin No. 268   Standard Oil Company of Indiana   Cut No. 850

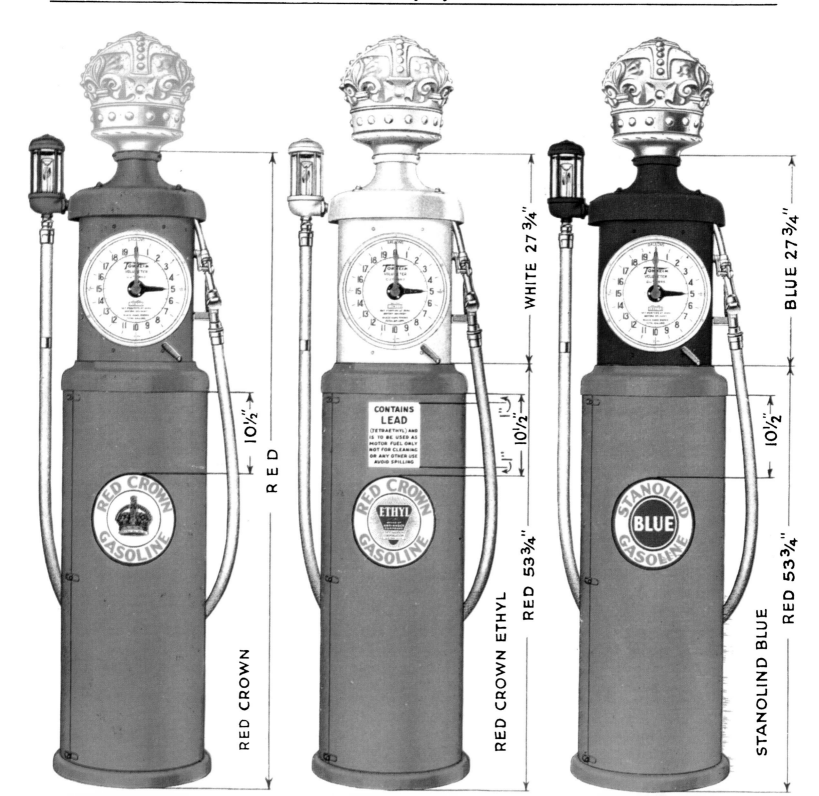

Chapter 4

Wipe the Windows and Check the Oil, 1933–1936

Remember how when we pulled into a service station our automobile tires were always greeted by the familiar ding-ding of the driveway air hose? Those were the days when attendants still checked under the hood and attitudes were friendlier. Employees still had a personality, and gasoline companies an image the public could identify with. You could "trust your car to the man who wears the Star" and always count on the Flying Red Horse to guide your way in the dark of night to an open gasoline station. Friendly full service was the common credo of the roadside refueling stop, a place where all motorists in need could find the goods and services required to keep their vehicles running, wherever their travels might take them.

Maybe It Was All a Dream

In the early thirties, a new way of life was emerging in every city and town linked with the roadways, powered by the exponential rise of new retail outlets selling refined motor fuel. In America's continuing love affair with the automobile, those were exciting days. Gas could be bought for pennies, with full service included. Free glasses and promotional prizes were passed out to all. Promising to load our oversized trunks to the hilt with electric toasters and modern conveniences, small rectangular tickets filled our glove compartments.

Gasoline pumps "talked" to us with a friendly ring at gallon intervals and signs advertised the price per gallon with fewer than three digits. Hubcaps adorned the walls and a sense of innocence and wonder permeated the roadside. In the highway game show known as *We Want Your Business,* everyone was a winner. With the automobile deeply rooted in all aspects of culture, American society was hopelessly infatuated with four-wheeled transportation and the consumption of huge quantities of gasoline. The magical lure of the roadway and the good life it promised was too strong to resist. A visit to the local gasoline service station was a trip in itself, a social ritual.

Selling Gallons of It

After World War I, America took to the nation's roadways in vast numbers. By 1925, affordable automobiles and decent roads had become commonplace. To supply the perceived demand, oil companies produced tremendous amounts of fuel and overexpanded through their gasoline stations. Rationing for the war effort was a thing of the past and gasoline soon became available in overwhelming quantities.

To help defray some of the costs of marketing fuel, many gasoline stations were leased to dealers by the end of 1929. Hoping that the independent operators could absorb the price cuts needed to beat the competition, the major

Tokheim Oil Tank & Pump Company product bulletin. Cut No. 850 Volumeter, Circa 1930. *Tokheim Corporation*

"Fuel Oil Distribution" and "Service Station Management" were once courses offered in New York City's vocational high schools. It wasn't that easy to wipe a windshield clean; the job had to be done just right, with a flair and grace that would keep the customers coming back to purchase more gasoline and have their cars serviced. By 1931, gasoline station owners discovered that the way to fortune was to cater in every possible way to the comfort and convenience of the motorist. No service was too big or small as windows were wiped, oil levels checked, tires aired up, radiators topped off and batteries checked. The full-service gasoline station was in business to please the motoring customer. *Cities Service Company*

oil refiners gladly made the shift from their company-owned outlets. Unfortunately, with two cents from each gallon of gas sold going to pay for rent and utilities, the six cents per gallon margin the dealers operated within didn't allow for much of a cushion to turn a profit.

To increase station income in this atmosphere of competition and overproduction, oil refiners set upon the task of improving products and services. Research to upgrade gasoline moved ahead in hopes of producing higher-quality fuels to outsell and outperform the competition's current brand. Advanced motor oils were developed to operate at higher temperatures and under more extreme conditions.

Helpful practices at the pump ushered in an era of full service as courtesy tasks like cleaning the windshield and checking tire pressure be-

At the Sinclair service station of the thirties, station attendants acted as representatives for the good of the customer. Here, two women are advised on the pros and cons of using a certain brand of motor oil and given written information on its particular advantages. Like the local police officer walking a beat downtown, the station attendant commanded a certain respect when it came to making decisions about what would go into a motorcar. *Atlantic Richfield Company*

came standard. Mechanical repair and chassis lubrication was being added too, as the drive-through filling station evolved into a true "service station."

The cutthroat competition existing between the major oil companies and the independents in this hectic period of large-volume gasoline production and chaotic price wars caused sales tactics to evolve into much more than simple peddling. They had to; by 1933, more than 170,000 gasoline stations were doing business in the United States. Selling refined petroleum to the motorist had developed into an art form. To some of its most devoted

Bruce Barton, an influential spokesman for this new philosophy of sales, addressed a gathering of prominent American oil people in 1928 with a motivational talk extolling The Magic of

No matter how small the town or how unpopulated, station owners were proud of their gasoline stations and eager to pose for photographs. At this 105th Street service station, chassis lubrication, two grades of gasoline and Coca-Cola were eagerly offered up to the motorist.
Shell Oil Company

Gasoline. With an exuberance still dizzy from the general prosperity of the Roaring Twenties, his speech hoped to convince the business world just how alive the sales spirit in that hopeful era was:

"Stand for an hour beside one of your filling stations. Talk to the people who come in to buy gas. Discover for yourself what magic a dollar's worth of gasoline a week has worked in their lives.

"My friends, it is the juice of the fountain of eternal youth that you are selling. It is health. It is comfort. It is success. And you have sold merely a bad smelling liquid at so many cents per gallon. You have never lifted it out of the category of a hated expense. It is an item for father to grumble about in the family budget. It is something for

mother to economize on, though she has to drive five miles out of her way to save a cent a gallon.

"There is a magnificent place for imagination in your business, but you must get it on the other side of the pump. You must put yourself in the place of the man and woman in whose lives your gasoline has worked miracles."

Many station operators endeavored to do just that as every conceivable effort was made to find out exactly what the motoring public really cared about, especially when it came to selecting and purchasing gasoline. After careful analysis, it was no surprise to discover that the public felt most favorable toward gasoline service stations that looked presentable and portrayed an overall image of quality and reliability. With all the other countless operations hawking gasoline along the

At the Udina Triangle in 1931, Stanolind Blue cost twelve cents per gallon. Since a Nehi cost only five cents, choosing between an extra half gallon of gasoline and a refreshing cold drink was often difficult. *Edward Wesemann, Jr.*

General Petroleum integrated classical elements into its house designs during the late twenties and early thirties. Canopy pillars in this unusual design held small display cases able to enclose a range of assorted automotive merchandise and accessories. Restroom facilities were located in a separate structure near the rear of the lot, complete with latticework screens and white trellises typical of any suburban garden. *Arizona Historical Society, Tucson*

Constructed in 1929 and still pumping gas more than sixty years later, Dennis Oluasen's Shell station and convenience mart strives to serve customers the old-fashioned way. The station stands in the shadow of Mt. Rainier at Enumclaw, Washington.

A sampling of typical Texaco station materials, including oils and lubricants, and restroom signs.

roadside, a successful gasoline station and its employees had to look smart, crisp and well-groomed.

The typical grease monkey who spent most of the time in lubrication pits changing oil and greasing bearings certainly was not the proper image to present to the fickle public. A service representative the public could trust with the upkeep of their automobiles had to command a certain respect, to project a level of pride and know-how that enabled him or her to do a job right, the first time.

Dress for Success

A highly visible employee, the station attendant was effectively an extension of the brand of gasoline sold and ultimately a figure head for the petroleum company that produced that product. The employee's appearance had to instill a sense of quality and service in the minds of motorists to ensure their future return for business. The typical caricature of mechanic

A classic metal-clad structure like the type built for Texas Company during its campaign to standardize stations, Billy's Service Station has all the elements of streamlined design. Every weekend, classic restored vehicles line up streetside to drive through and take part in the retro-atmosphere of Billy's nostalgic service station. Like pump attendants who worked at filling stations during the heyday of America's gas consumption, the gas jockeys at Billy's wear a black bowtie as part of their basic uniform; the same tie was once an integral element of the attendant's dress code and a large part of the company's service image. Vic Huber

Inside the office at Billy's, many unique treasures that rekindle past memories can be examined. Advertising art and photographs relating to the refueling of automobiles line the walls. A Coca-Cola machine in mint condition and a pink neon dealership clock are just two of the nostalgic items that cause one to say, "Hey, I remember that!" Vic Huber

Billy's Service Station

A neverending ritual begins as vintage automobiles pack the boulevard in the pursuit of girls, rock-and-roll and the perfect cruising strip.

Over the distant calm of the Pacific, a hue of burnt sienna paints the horizon as the sun's journey from its zenith nears completion, creating room for the languor of dusk's arrival. In acknowledgment of the night and in almost perfect synchronization, four-wheeled machines shoot down Anaheim Boulevard and nearby side streets in search of their familiar groove. In an orchestrated nod of agreement, the stars show their stuff. Restored hot rods and stock street vehicles begin jockeying for their position in the streetside pecking order. Like modern-day gladiators heading into bat-

tle, they roar down the boulevard into the neon fray.

As they slow to check out the action on the sidewalk, the rumble of glass-packs and screeching of tires mix with the Chuck Berry and Bo Diddley guitar licks spilling from car speakers, creating a uniquely nostalgic cacophony of sounds. Like chromed contestants in a beauty contest, cars flash by with grilles like grinning faces, in step with the beat.

In the crazed bumper-to-bumper queue, warm trailers of light paint the canvas of darkness as cars begin flashing their brakes. Repeating images of liquid light scroll across moving glass, the curved surfaces of polished automobiles mirroring the fluorescent images of the roadside. Up ahead, the warm glow of neon tubing radiates into the air, bouncing off enameled steel. Like a beacon from another time, the neon signage of Billy's Service Station lights a contemporary mirage, radiating the values of yesterday with its image. Electrified by this apparition from the past, the urban tarmac is rippling with life.

It's still hard for some of the locals to believe that this architectural "blast from the past" is the same greasy building Bill Taormina purchased just a few years ago. Covered with ugly flagstones back then, its true character was hidden from the urban passerby. After discovering its hidden identity, Bill quickly became obsessed with the restoration of the structure, meticulously removing the stones with all the excitement of an archaeological dig. Beneath, treasure was revealed: a prefabricated all-metal gas station, circa 1930. With the help of petroliana collectors across the country, he obtained the original items needed to restore the structure and infused a pronounced fifties ambience into the project.

Now, Billy's is the centerpiece for the entire boulevard. Eager attendants outfitted in snappy white shirts, black caps and bow ties stand ready, waiting to serve. Beneath the canopy, pumps topped with illuminated globes hawk long-defunct brands of gasoline. A single service bay reserved for servicing and greasing houses repair equipment and a colorful collection of porcelain advertising signs. Inside the office, a friendly Coke machine greets customers with its icy refreshments. Framed paper ephemera and nostalgic photos of all types grace the walls, surrounding a classic clock rimmed in pink neon. Outside, a yellow visible-register pump stands sentinel over the parking lot, watching traffic as it passes.

Luckily, local merchants liked the classy overtones of Streamline Moderne used at the station and agreed to follow the lead of Billy's, rebuilding their storefronts in the same nostalgic style. Now, a section of town once considered rundown is slowly being transformed into an architectural gateway of timeless grace and beauty.

Because one man with imagination looked to the past for the secrets it held, this long strip of asphalt in southern California is now alive with images from the fifties, every night of the week. Igniting a neighborhood reawakening, Bill's station restoration project has inadvertently become the catalyst for the revitalization of Anaheim Boulevard. Check the oil, wipe the windows and fill 'er up—at Billy's Service Station, it's 1956 once again!

Utilized at Standard Oil Company of New York service stations throughout the United States before metal and paper cans were widely adopted, this Socony-Vacuum oil bottle holder complete with six bottles and matching spouts is a valuable find for the petroliana collector.

with ill-fitting clothing covered in grease stains with oil-soaked rag hanging out of rear pocket was an image oil companies desperately desired to improve.

Like their well-dressed counterparts in the military, the gasoline station attendants had to be on their toes at all times. In the competitive world of petroleum marketing, the representative who went out to greet cars and refill gasoline tanks had to maintain a high standard of personal hygiene. Along with product, the public was buying an image—a certain style that said "We're here to help you and give you the best in products and services that money can buy." By sheer business necessity, conformity of style became the guideline for increased sales and customer attraction. It wasn't long before most oil companies and independents required station employees to wear standard uniforms.

At a number of Shell Oil Company's thirties gasoline stations, service personnel sported leather shoes shined to perfection with matching leather shin guards. Jodhpurs, a matching waist-length jacket, a long-sleeve shirt and a crisp black bow tie were typical attire. On the jacket's breast pocket, station affiliation was displayed proudly with a metal pin or fabric patch shaped like the company's insignia. Influenced heavily by the style of military uniforms, the Shell uniform included a hat typical of any service hat. Decorated with the same company identification as the jacket, it allowed immediate brand recognition during times when a station worker interacted personally with the public.

Some oil companies went with more relaxed styles at their sales outlets and utilized the basic white jumpsuit as uniform. Covering the legs, arms and major portions of the body, it was the perfect shell for protection against grease and dirt. Soft caps made from the same white fabric covered the head and kept dirt and rust from falling onto the scalp while working beneath an automobile. Easily maintained and inexpensive to purchase, both could be decorated with company symbols and the names of the attendants who wore them, further personalizing service. The classic black bow tie applied to this style too, completing the standard dress code.

Industrial supply companies offered a wide range of uniform styles in wool, cotton and later durable rayon to the large number of petroleum marketers and independent station owners. Advertisements in industry magazines such as the *National Petroleum News* touted the virtues of these new uniforms and their benefits:

"To management this means smart-looking employees—men and women who will reflect a smart organization. To customers . . . the pleasure of dealing with neat looking representatives. To the worker himself . . . the satisfaction and pride of knowing that he is perfectly "suited" for the job. And finally to the housewife who does the washing . . . the knowledge that work clothes made of Reeves Army Twill will stay fresh, crisp and new looking washing-after-washing."

Perpetuating the Full-Service Myth

Of course, gasoline stations would have to rely on more than just nattily attired gas jockeys who dispensed motor fuel to pull in the business. The simple mechanical services needed to maintain an automobile at its optimum performance levels would have to be taken care of, too. That meant making sure motorists could see through their windshield clearly as they drove out of the station, their mind assured that the tires were properly inflated, the crankcase was topped off to the proper level and the radiator was full of the fluid that cooled the engine.

Once the valued customer arrived at the pumps, snappy attendants went to work on the waiting vehicle to make sure all these services were performed. Immediately, tires were checked for proper inflation pressure to ensure the safety of the vehicle and the customer's later return. By use of an inflation hose at the pump island attached to a remote compressor, the job was easily taken care of. Dispensed free of charge to the customer, air was always available—whether the patron decided to purchase gasoline or not.

Small yellow machines installed at today's convenience stores for the purchase of air would have been considered ludicrous by yesterday's service station standards. The concept that one should pay for a commodity so basic to human existence was unthinkable in the days when America's gasoline stations were fighting for business. The customer was of prime impor-

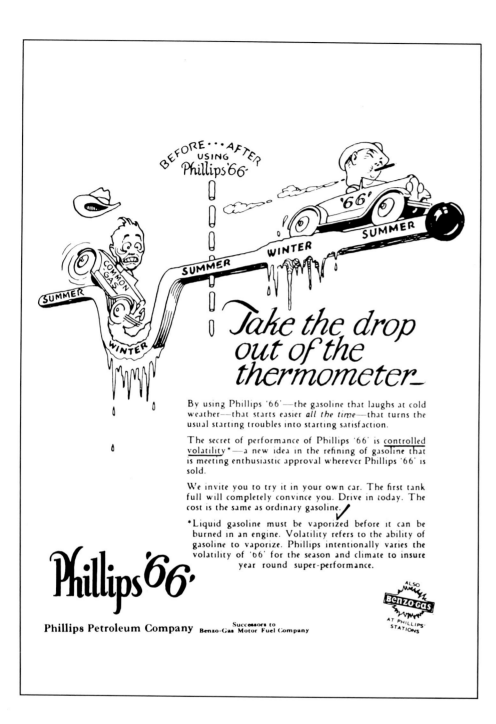

Take the drop out of the thermometer advertisement for Phillips 66 controlled volatility gasoline. Courtesy Phillips Petroleum Company

order of business. With a flick of the wrist, the vehicle's hood was popped open and the oil dipstick gingerly removed from the hot engine for inspection. A quick swipe with an industrial shop cloth stored within the attendant's rear pocket cleared the way for proper measurement of oil level. If it was low, the attendant informed the customer and offered various brands of motor oils that could be quickly dispensed at the drive-through.

If the customer requested it, detailed advice regarding lubricant viscosity and the type best suited for particular driving habits was freely given. After all, the service station attendant's job was to help motorists enjoy their driving to the fullest and to make sure the public knew what modern petroleum products could do for their vehicle. Working at a gas station was more than a job—it meant being a personal consultant for the public's total enjoyment of the automobile.

Dispensing with Pride

In 1931, the Standard Oil Company of Indiana's brands included Iso-Vis for twenty cents per quart, Polarine for fifteen cents and Stanolind (for Standard Oil of Indiana) for ten cents. After the proper selection was made by the customer with the service attendant's assistance, a sixty-gallon Highboy Lubester dispensed oil in quart or gallon measures, all pumped by hand.

Glass bottles holding one quart of oil were stored in eight-bottle racks usually located at both sides of the pump island in front of the station building. From the tall rectangular oil dispenser, lubricant filled the fragile containers. An arrow pointer and the lettering Fill To This Line in raised glass relief denoted the proper fill level on the decanters.

Often, spring steel inserts located near their necks indicated the viscosity number and the brand they contained. Some bottles had brand names embossed directly into the glass; others were marked with oil company logo or trademark decals identifying brand names. Oil was poured directly from these containers into the automobile, and then the containers were returned to their rack empty for later use and refilling.

tance in the battle for revenues, and everything that could be done to associate good service with a particular brand of gasoline was tried. Selling air was not one of them.

With tires filled to their proper pressure, the typical station attendant moved on to the next

With the oil level and tire pressure checked, the station attendant would move on to the main reason a car had pulled in: gasoline. At a typical Standard station such as Edward Wesemann's Udina Triangle, forty miles west of Chicago, three grades of gasoline were offered for general sale. The premium gasoline sold for fifteen cents per gallon and was purchased by those who desired better engine performance. Containing tetra-ethyl lead (a poisonous metallic compound) to help impede the engine knock of low-compression motors, this high-test Solite was a popular brand for those who could afford it. A typical sale amounted to only five gallons during the Depression, with ten gallons or more going to luxury cars or trucks.

The regular grade of gasoline was known as Red Crown Ethyl and was usually purchased in one or two gallon increments by motorists who were less financially secure. At fourteen cents a gallon it might have been considered a bargain by today's standards, yet was still too expensive for many motorists of the era.

For the poorest drivers, a "fighting" brand sold under the name Stanolind Blue allowed the station attendant to pump enough gas into their cars to get them where they were going for only twelve cents per gallon. Oil companies introduced fighting grades of gasoline in the early thirties to compete with the private-brand discounters selling fuel directly from the tank car to trackside autos.

Peddling Gasoline and Gimmicks

During the visible-register pump's reign at America's filling stations, gasoline grades were easy to distinguish by the ordinary motorist. Dyes were often added to a station's underground storage tanks to color each type of motor fuel with a different hue, making visual grade identification from behind the windshield possible.

The large West Coast gasoline independent known as the Gilmore Oil Company sold the Blu-Green brand of gasoline from its visible pumps. Recognized from southern California to Seattle by its baying lion and Roar with Gilmore motto, it made good use of the coloring technique. Many other petroleum refiners used the

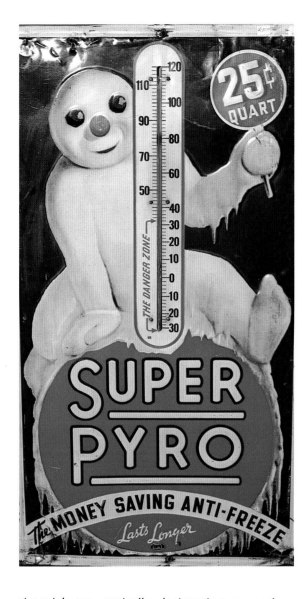

Super-Pyro, the money-saving antifreeze. Tin sign on display at the General Petroleum Museum in 1989.

gimmick too, typically designating an amber cast to signify regular gasoline or the cheapest grade sold. A red or blue coloring usually identified premium gas, with a clear, colorless liquid often reserved for utility fuels sold to farm equipment owners.

The hype connected with the merchandising of gasoline was not limited to the coloring of gasoline grades. Oil companies continually developed new additives and gasoline types, many made with secret chemical additives or revolutionary refining processes and techniques. All claimed superior performance and quality,

Tokheim Oil Tank & Pump Company product bulletin. Cut No. 605 Interior View. Circa 1926. *Tokheim Corporation*

Next page
Shell Minnesota road map, circa 1929. In 1914, Gulf Oil Company took the suggestion of local Pittsburgh advertiser William B. Akin and mailed a map of Allegheny County, Pennsylvania, to more than 10,000 registered motorists. Later, other maps were offered free through the mail and at gas station outlets nationwide. In a short time, most major oil companies offered free maps as part of their station services. *Mike Parsons Collection*

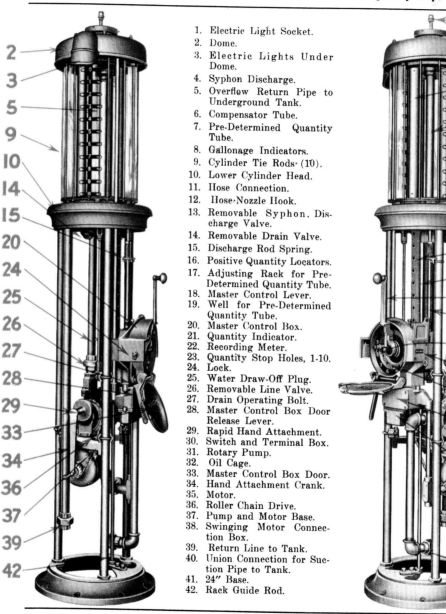

Interior View of Cut 605
Electric Motor Driven Ten-Gallon Capacity Visible Gasoline Dispenser
Equipped With Master Control and Positive Pre-Determine Quantity Stops

1. Electric Light Socket.
2. Dome.
3. Electric Lights Under Dome.
4. Syphon Discharge.
5. Overflow Return Pipe to Underground Tank.
6. Compensator Tube.
7. Pre-Determined Quantity Tube.
8. Gallonage Indicators.
9. Cylinder Tie Rods (10).
10. Lower Cylinder Head.
11. Hose Connection.
12. Hose Nozzle Hook.
13. Removable Syphon. Discharge Valve.
14. Removable Drain Valve.
15. Discharge Rod Spring.
16. Positive Quantity Locators.
17. Adjusting Rack for Pre-Determined Quantity Tube.
18. Master Control Lever.
19. Well for Pre-Determined Quantity Tube.
20. Master Control Box.
21. Quantity Indicator.
22. Recording Meter.
23. Quantity Stop Holes, 1-10.
24. Lock.
25. Water Draw-Off Plug.
26. Removable Line Valve.
27. Drain Operating Bolt.
28. Master Control Box Door Release Lever.
29. Rapid Hand Attachment.
30. Switch and Terminal Box.
31. Rotary Pump.
32. Oil Cage.
33. Master Control Box Door.
34. Hand Attachment Crank.
35. Motor.
36. Roller Chain Drive.
37. Pump and Motor Base.
38. Swinging Motor Connection Box.
39. Return Line to Tank.
40. Union Connection for Suction Pipe to Tank.
41. 24″ Base.
42. Rack Guide Rod.

Tokheim Oil Tank and Pump Company
FORT WAYNE, INDIANA, U. S. A.
Offices in Principal Cities

1929
SHELL ROAD MAP
MINNESOTA
Super-
SHELL
GASOLINE
400
"EXTRA DRY"
SHELL
MOTOR
OIL
SHELL GASOLINE
SHELL MOTOR OIL
SHELL
GASOLINE
Compliments of
JANESVILLE OIL CO.
Janesville, Minn.

sometimes making it difficult for a motorist unschooled in the science of chemistry to discern exactly what was flowing into the automobile's tank.

With a team of research scientists at General Motors, Dr. Thomas Midgley and Charles F. Kettering developed an important gasoline additive. By installing a quartz window in the side of an engine cylinder, they saw visual clues to the cause of engine ping by watching the fuel burn. Experimenting with numerous chemicals, the group discovered that when small quantities of tetraethyl lead were added to gasoline, a decrease in detonation or "knocking" would result.

General Motors and Standard Oil Company of New Jersey joined to form the Ethyl Gasoline Corporation in 1924 and introduced the fuel additive to the public under the Ethyl name. A number of oil companies quickly contracted its use in their gasolines, and soon a variety of

premium-priced antiknock motor fuels contained the compound. Thanks to the high-octane fuels that resulted, automobile manufacturers could easily increase efficiency in combustion engines by designing motors with higher compression—without worrying about the problems of detonation limiting their design.

The Gulf Oil Company developed a method of cracking high-boiling crudes (extracting gasoline from heavier oils) with aluminum chloride in the twenties and marketed the resulting gasoline under the No-Nox brand. Sweet smelling and white like water, this gasoline possessed superior antiknock properties and was regarded as the best antidetonation fuel available before the widespread use of tetraethyl lead additives.

One of the first companies in the industry to produce gasoline by this method of catalytic cracking, Gulf heralded the fuel's virtues in a thirties Info-map given free to its gasoline customers: "Gulf No-Nox gasoline is a high antiknock motor-fuel that no regular gasoline can touch for quality. It makes your engine run quieter and better [and] gives full mileage . . . plus smoother, more trouble-free performance. Ask for Gulf No-Nox today!"

The Red Grange Football Contest, circa 1936, invited fans to outguess Red Grange on scores. A Babe Ruth contest gave away free cars, with entry blanks available at stations in 1937. Sinclair Motor Oil's ads of 1932 were demure and understated. By 1934, a self-confident stance emerged with ads signed by Harry Sinclair himself. *Atlantic Richfield Company*

Shell Illinois road map, circa 1932. *Mike Parsons Collection*

Tokheim Oil Tank & Pump Company product bulletin. Cut No. 850 Twin Volumeter. Circa 1930. *Tokheim Corporation*

Charles Lindbergh used Mobiloil B in his *Spirit of St. Louis* on the first-ever solo flight across the Atlantic in 1927. Standard Oil Company of New York still utilized the red Gargoyle logo for brand identification back then, before the merger with Vacuum Oil Company in 1931. When the two companies joined, the Flying Red Horse—first used by a Japanese affiliate in 1925—was adopted as the worldwide corporate symbol as stations were standardized. *Courtesy Mobil Corporation*

The Phillips Petroleum Company introduced Phillips 66 gasoline in 1927 and touted its "controlled volatility" and superior blending that enabled it to burn well in both winter and summer temperatures. Later in the thirties, the company's quest for a superior aviation fuel and its early work in polymerization (a process that combines hydrocarbon molecules of little value to form more complex molecules with high volatility) led to the introduction of Phillips Poly-Gas. Utilizing a parrot and the familiar 66 logo to get the motorist's attention, 1937 advertising copy trumpeted the instant-starting characteristics of this new high-test fuel:

"You tip-toe the button, and there is no missing . . . sputtering . . . or backfiring. What a kick! when your motor rolls over with no gnashing of teeth, purr-r-r-s into instant action, warms up fast. Besides, you save miles usually wasted by excessive use of the choke with ordinary low-test fuels."

Sinclair Motor Oil kept up the tradition in the fifties with its Power-X brand of gasoline. A new superpremium motor fuel, it was widely advertised as being "power-primed with rocket-fuel." By using a new X-chemical additive, Sinclair claimed the gasoline would help reduce the preignition problems of automobile engines, which occur when combustion chamber deposits become hot and cause a portion of the gasoline to ignite prematurely. Advertisements featured fanciful Buck Rogers-type vehicles streaking away from the pumps, fully loaded with the advanced fuel.

Later, Sinclair ads cajoled the car owner to "put new dinosaur power in your engine with nickel." Claiming its new oxidant inhibitor was ten times more effective than other antigum additives, the new nickel ingredient promised to fight harmful engine deposits. With its continuous use, engine wear could be reduced up to twenty-nine percent, allowing big savings on repair and replacements.

Strangely enough, other refining companies were developing metal deactivators that promised to protect gasoline from the effect of picking up metals in an automobile's fuel system. The confusion about additives and exactly what function they performed would continue for years.

Phill-up and Fly

Free 5 Gallons of Phillips '66'

—to introduce this new winter gasoline

Phillips '66'   Five Gallons Free

Flying was a national craze in the late twenties and served as the ideal theme to advertise Phillips Petroleum Company's new "easier-starting" gasoline. Phill-up "and fly" was the slogan used to introduce the new gasoline to consumers. A coupon redeemable for 5 gallons of the new 66 gravity fuel was given away just for coming in and saying "Phill 'er up." The model for the aviatrix in the advertisement, Virginia Wilson of Wichita, was one of several young women selected for the campaign. With leather flying cap and jacket, flight goggles, jodhpurs and of course warm gloves, she hoped to capture the imagination of a public still awed by the trans-Atlantic feat of Lindbergh. *Courtesy Phillips Petroleum Company*

What Time Is My Gas?

New electric meter-type pumps replaced the visible-register units at many gas stations by the late twenties. Known as "clock-face" pumps, these round-dial units were first developed by L. O. and N. A. Carlson of Erie Meter Systems and eventually replaced the fragile glass tank for gasoline measurement. With new rotary suction pumps, gasoline could now be pumped at a much faster rate. Whether flowing at fifteen gallons per minute or just one drop at a time, the new pumpers boasted increased accuracy at all rates of flow. Advanced units such as the Tokheim Cut No. 850 Volumeter were much simpler to operate and safer than the hand-operated visible pumps.

The typical clock-face pump relied on two fourteen-inch counting dials to meaure fluid volume, one situated on each side of the pump. A large red pointer similar to the minute hand on a clock measured fractions of gallons. After the red pointer made a complete revolution on the dial, a bell signaled the customer that one gallon of gasoline was delivered. As subsequent gallons flowed through the metering system, the total gallons pumped were indicated by the incremental movement of a shorter black hand. Up to twenty gallons of gasoline could be measured this way on the large dial. In addition, a numerical counter set into the clock face made it easy for the station operator to keep track of total gallons sold per day.

To placate a motoring public weaned on the ability to see their gas and to satisfy requirements set forth by the Sealers of Weights and Measures, pump manufacturers incorporated

Hollywood stunt flyer Colonel Art Goebel was sponsored by Phillips Petroleum Company in an air race organized by the Dole Pineapple Company in 1927. Utilizing Phillips' new high-gravity aviation fuel exclusively, he easily flew the single-engine *Woolaroc* from Oakland to victory in Honolulu—picking up the prize check for $25,000. Here, Goebel readies for takeoff to perform skywriting duties. *Courtesy Phillips Petroleum Company*

Phillips Petroleum Company had a flair for the dramatic in its thirties advertising. Goebel entertained crowds by writing Phillips 66 in huge letters in the sky, while an associate kept in radio contact and touted Phillips products on the ground. The public loved to watch the exploits of this touring daredevil and reciprocated by purchasing fuel for their own ground-level flights. *Courtesy Phillips Petroleum Company*

features to make the transition from visible register to dial metering less traumatic. Tokheim utilized a side-mounted Tele-gauge that incorporated a small glass crucible—almost exactly replicating the visible-register tank—at reduced scale. Connected to the side of the pump with a refueling hose dropping from its bottom, a center-mounted spinner inside the glass visibly indicated the flow of gasoline into the car. As fuel surged from the pump and traveled through the sight glass, small fanlike appendages twirled.

Friendly Roadside Beacons

The practice of mounting illuminated glass globes to help the customer identify gasoline brands and grades continued atop the new gas pumps. Whereas the earliest of these illuminated beacons simply advertised Gasolene or Filtered Gasoline, many oil companies designed and installed a number of visually distinctive globes by the thirties, using a variety of attention-getting graphics. As part of the overall campaign to have the motorist more readily associate their name with petroleum products, they proceeded

Shell Oil of California staged elaborate treasure hunts during the late twenties. Company-owned stations were decked out to promote the contest, with attendants dressed in full pirate regalia and a huge treasure chest atop the roof. *Shell Oil Company*

to mount these appealing globes on gas pumps nationwide.

In the late thirties, Stanley Wilson, advertising manager for an early Shell Oil Company division, designed a one-piece shell-shaped globe that soon became a familiar fixture on Shell's pumps in the United States and in countries overseas. When seeing it on the roadside, it was hard not to notice the bright red lettering of the word Shell embossed on the frosted glass,

informing the passing motorist that the station was open and ready for business—eager and willing to pump gasoline.

Standard Oil of Indiana introduced idealized versions of a regal crown for its pumps and fashioned them from heavy white milk glass. Lending an aura of quality and grace to the utilitarian machines they topped, these majestic globes were intended to conjure up images of royalty and tradition for all who viewed them in their roadside courts. Finished in different color schemes to signify various grades of gasoline, they were all easily recognizable. It was easy for the motorist to figure out which pump at a Standard station delivered Red Crown Ethyl gasoline—his majesty was easily identified by a solid white crown.

Phillips Petroleum Company borrowed the shape of a highway symbol normally used for depicting national routes on road maps for its distinctive globe. Originally conceived as a trade symbol for the company's superior motor fuel, the orange and black shield that took its place atop Phillips' pumps all across America was an icon already deeply embedded into the mind of any car owner who had ever planned a cross-country trip or read a roadside highway marker. Fashioned in thick three-dimensional glass, it proudly proclaimed the Phillips 66 brand of gasoline in living color. To loyal customers already familiar with the brand and to drivers contemplating its use, it was a friendly sight along many of the country's roadways.

Hooking Them with Treasure

The automobile service station is and always has been ideally suited for staging events designed to draw in the motorist from the fast track. Almost always constructed in a place of prominence or a location where many passing vehicles can see it, the gas station is inherently a highly visible roadside business. Practically everyone who owns a car requires gasoline sooner or later and will eventually need to stop at a station in order to continue traveling. That part of motoring is an accepted necessity—the chance of getting something free or having some fun at the same time is just icing on the cake.

Shell Oil of California came to those same conclusions back in the late twenties and dreamed up the concept of staging elaborate treasure hunts that promised to satiate the public's universal longing for buried riches. The prosperity of the early twenties had reached its peak and all in America were ready to get their share of the wealth. Hundreds of hopeful treasure hunters converged on the numerous West Coast cities staging the highly publicized events, including San Jose and Seattle.

Bearing picks, shovels and pitchforks, mad throngs arrived in vehicles of all descriptions in order to reserve their privilege to dig and scrape through layers of earth; yet only a few would go home winners. Held back by ropes cordoning off the designated treasure zone, excited contestants waited to stampede across the barrier like a herd of cattle when the signal was sounded by a company official. With wild abandon reminiscent of the California gold rush of 1849, they combed every last cubic foot of earth until all hidden treasures were revealed. Carefully placed beneath the surface, small plaster of Paris shells filled with certificates redeemable for merchandise were discovered.

Shell's company-owned stations were decked out for maximum promotion of the contest and didn't miss a trick in exciting the mind and imagination of the gasoline customer. To help would-be treasure seekers with their search, mysterious "clew slips" were given out to enthusiastic motorists interested in joining the upcoming festivities. Station buildings were adorned with the skull and crossbones of the Jolly Roger with the words Pirate Treasure Hunt emblazoned in paint across the roof overhang. A mock treasure chest of immense proportions sat in a place of prominence atop the roof as station attendants dressed as pirates went about their business servicing vehicles and pumping gas. For the automobile owner just passing by, it was hard not to be intrigued with the happenings.

Sharing the Christmas Spirit

Following in the success of the buried-treasure promotion, Christmas-theme exhibits were installed by Shell Oil Company at prime station locations in order to bolster sagging sales during the slowest part of the holiday season in 1929. From their back-seat viewpoint, children were entranced by the magic they witnessed through the rear window. In turn, they would influence their gasoline-buying parents to drive in the next time they drove by. With no admission charge or lengthy trip required to get there, few denied their youngsters the treat. While the sometimes uneventful task of having the family car filled with gasoline was underway, even the grown-ups could have some fun.

Awaiting the signal from a company official to begin the hunt, Depression-era treasure seekers were eager to start. Certificates redeemable for merchandise and prizes were hidden inside small plaster of Paris shells, with only a few of the large crowd going away winners. *Shell Oil Company*

At Fell and Stanyan streets in San Francisco, a snow-covered rendition of Mt. Shasta created a surreal backdrop for the small prefab station house positioned near its base. A huge model ten times larger than the diminutive office and pumps, it was illuminated at night and highly visible. Rendering the largest billboards of the time to the stature of small signs, it rose up from the roadside, an apparition constructed solely to steal attention from any other stations in close proximity. For nighttime motorists approaching from various directions, it was a sight to behold.

The Christmas displays became more complex and reached the pinnacle of their extravagance in 1930. Installed at the same busy location as the California mountain, a full-sized fantasy-scape of Toytown was erected that year. Stretching over a distance of two city blocks, it was constructed for the unheard-of cost of $40,000. Considering that it was only used for the short Christmas season and that America was in the middle of the greatest depression in its history, it was regarded as an amazing expense by competitors and customers alike.

Despite the costs, the outlandish displays proved to be a tremendous success with the buying public. The entire country was searching for something different to help people take their mind off their financial woes; for the lucky residents of the West, a visit to Toytown or some other larger-than-life attraction was just the tonic required.

With the large increase in business they produced, the flamboyant Christmas installations paid for themselves many times over. In only one day of sales during the 1929 holiday season, the hectic station at Fell and Stanyan streets pumped over 12,000 gallons of Shell's gasoline into hundreds of motorists' tanks. Since the average gas station in that general area typically sold the same amount of fuel in a month, it was agreed that the Christmas displays were doing something right and evoking the hoped-for response: an increase in overall sales and customer interest in Shell products.

Opening on a Grand Scale

A new gasoline station opening for business offered tremendous possibilities for publicity promotions and events to spark customer interest. With colorful banners, clowns, giveaway premiums and pretty girls, grand openings helped get out the word that a new station was opening for business in town. By employing a select sampling of show business tactics and borrowing a handful of P. T. Barnum's old tricks, first-day productions could be staged on a shoestring budget, with acceptable results.

At many of Shell Oil Company's midcontinent grand openings in 1934, a complement of a dozen Shell Girls welcomed new customers and presented ladies with beautiful orchids. This event was definitely for the adults, with searchlights casting their beams on newly constructed station buildings in what looked much like a Hollywood opening night.

As a long procession of motorized curiosity seekers arrived to admire the sights at one such opening, the musical stylings of the St. Louis Civic Band filled the Missouri air from the bandstand atop the station building. Company officials and station employees in formal attire mingled with families and friends in the cele-

brating crowd. Dressed in black tie and tails and foregoing any sort of protective jumpsuit, L. B. Veeder performed routine lubrication service on a waiting automobile. Crouched beneath tons of rubber and steel held high by the station's lift, he pumped the company's latest lubricant into grease fittings. Proving that the task wasn't necessarily a messy job, he seized the perfect opportunity to demonstrate the products and methods of the Shellubrication service he had a large part in developing for the company.

The Standard Oil Company of New York employed a children's horse ride fashioned after the likeness of its company mascot, Pegasus, for new-station grand openings during the fifties. Like the coin-operated arcade horses found at amusement parlors and later in shopping center walkways, it was powered by an electric motor and gave a small child a quick ride in the Old West by way of its up-and-down rocking motion. A marketing representative dressed in full western regalia snapped photographs and presided over the rodeo as parents were enlisted to sign up for company credit cards. Five of these portable units toured new openings around the country and were corralled at one specific stop for only a short period to facilitate maximum exposure and publicity.

Enchanted by the gallant red steed and its mechanized movements, children begged their

Shell Oil Company's Christmas exhibits were installed to attract the children riding in passing cars. Hopefully, parents influenced by the youngsters' pleas to pull over would purchase a few gallons of gasoline, since they were already there. *Shell Oil Company*

Passing out free prizes for the kids, this Phillips "grand opening girl" helps to make another station event a success in the company's Florida sales region. When the kids in the back seat are happy, they get along with each other and play quietly, making it easier for Mom and Dad to navigate through traffic and get to their destination safely. Is it any wonder free prizes were geared mostly toward children? *Courtesy Phillips Petroleum Company*

Next page
Phillips Petroleum Company used the grand opening as a perfect occasion to give away promotional items and free prizes to the gasoline-purchasing car owner during the fifties. Posing in front of a Phillips service station constructed in the eye-grabbing style of the exaggerated modem, President Boots Adams (who started out as a Phillips shipping clerk at the age of 21) and Vice President of Sales E. H. "Ted" Lyons kick off another station grand opening. With assistance from a pair of clowns wearing Phillips 66 pajamas, they offer free gifts and trinkets to customers. Station events like this helped to introduce products and services available at Phillips stations. *Courtesy Phillips Petroleum Company*

parents in command of the wheel to pull over and allow them a short ride. To take part in the festivities, the family would drive in and perhaps purchase a few gallons of gasoline. Whether fuel was purchased or not, many future customers were introduced to the speed and power of the Flying Red Horse at an early age by the rides. They would never forget the happy experience of taming the sky while riding horseback at the newest Socony station. Someday, they would make the transition from bicycle to motor vehicle—and it was hoped that the fond memories of their youthful ride would then be conjured forth automatically every time they passed the sign of the Flying Red Horse.

Chapter 5

New Images for New Gas Stations, 1937–1946

During the economic downturn between 1929 and 1932, the national income of the United States was reduced by over fifty percent, with some 2.5 million cars and trucks left to stand idle. Suddenly, the giddy times of high-volume gasoline station sales and immense profits enjoyed during the Roaring Twenties slowed. The hordes of motorists who once streamed into filling stations in long lines were reduced to more moderate bands, detoured by the warning signs of the Great Depression. Now, a large segment of the population had a hard time feeding themselves, reserving what little money they could earn for basic survival necessities. Gasoline for the family automobile was still being purchased but in smaller quantities.

As the overall volume of motorists dropped off at the gas pump in 1930, dollar sales at the neighborhood filling station declined almost as fast as at the stock exchange. To make matters worse, the petroleum industry was soon flooded with large supplies of crude oil. A drilling rig in east Texas had punched into the largest oil field in petroleum history, capable of producing some 300,000 barrels of raw crude per day. Soon, a massive wave of cheap third-grade gasoline swamped the country. Unavoidably, gasoline prices quickly hit rock bottom, falling from the preceding year's 17.9 cents per gallon average to a low of ten cents per gallon in most major metropolitan areas.

Now more than ever before, the major oil company stations and smaller independent stations had to rely on products and services other than gasoline for revenues. To stay in the black, a wide range of automotive items had to be displayed and sold, including tires, batteries and accessories. Initially experimented with during the twenties, this stocking of secondary merchandise now demanded universal adoption by all gasoline station proprietors to make up for the losses created by the ailing economy.

The promotion of a simple chassis "lube job" and basic automotive repair services was quickly stepped up to bolster profits, too. Additional lubrication and mechanical bays were added to a long roster of gas stations as the latest in air-powered rotary lifts were installed to raise vehicles. To perform the work more efficiently, the proper tools and greasing equipment were purchased, as station attendants were trained to do the work. The Lubritorium was now a basic part of the American gasoline station, with the moneymaking services it generated a welcome boost to sagging fuel sales.

Teague's Texaco Box

The Texas Company (Texaco) had well over 40,000 gas stations in operation by the mid-thirties, with many long overdue for major upgrading. Building usefulness began to diminish dramatically as the new service and market-

Texaco magazine advertisement from 1952 promising Registered Rest Rooms wherever you drove "in all 48 States." *Texaco Inc.*

Next page
During the thirties, Gulf Oil Company constructed a number of architect-designed gasoline stations that featured multiple banks of gas pumps that allowed customers to pull up easily and have their tanks refilled. Finally, the horse-drawn tank wagon was replaced. Now, a more modern version of the tanker supplied by Mack Truck rolled on pneumatic tires and sported the latest in headlamp illumination. *Chevron Corporation*

ing features dictated by the depressed economy began to see full implementation. Inadequate window treatments made it difficult to effectively display oil, fan belts, tires, headlamps, batteries, specialty greases, cables, lamp bulbs and countless other accessories. The "add-on" lubrication bays hastily installed by many operators in the twenties didn't contain the space required to efficiently repair or lubricate vehicles properly,

either. A hybrid building design that could incorporate gasoline pumps, merchandise sales and automotive repair facilities all under one roof had become a necessity.

Industrial designer Walter Dorwin Teague understood Texaco's concerns about developing a new station prototype and was contracted by the company to come up with a new set of service station designs. With the strong belief

To harmonize with the Stanford University campus in California, this Palo Alto mission-style station was constructed in 1932. An elaborate version of the house bungalow, it employed elements of the Southwest in its use of red tile roofing and adobe finish. Two rows of Tokheim Cut No. 850 Volumeter gas pumps situated under the elaborate canopy offered premium Green Streak gasoline, Shell Regular and Shell Ethyl for sale. *Shell Oil Company*

By the mid-thirties, Shell station architecture mimicked the art deco designs of the company's San Francisco corporate office tower. One of the two new Shell stations built in Indianapolis in 1934, this particular model boasted a two-bay service area, a fully windowed office, a side-access restroom and an illuminated pump island display case. Mounted atop the clock-dial-indicator gasoline pumps sit the one-piece globes designed by Stanley Wilson, advertising manager for an early Shell division. *Shell Oil Company*

Patent drawings for Herbert O. Alden Art Deco station. *Shell Oil Company*

Next page
Partially influenced by the unadorned simplicity of the International Style, Walter Dorwin Teague presented a number of distinct station models to Texaco's board of directors by 1937. By use of rounded roof-lines and aerodynamic gas pumps mounted on smoothed islands, the new structures contained marked references to the Streamline Moderne. By 1940, over 500 of the new stations were built or remodeled to Teague's specifications. With all the precision of a modern machine, the gleaming white streamlined box was soon to become the newly exalted form of gasoline station architecture. *Texaco Inc.*

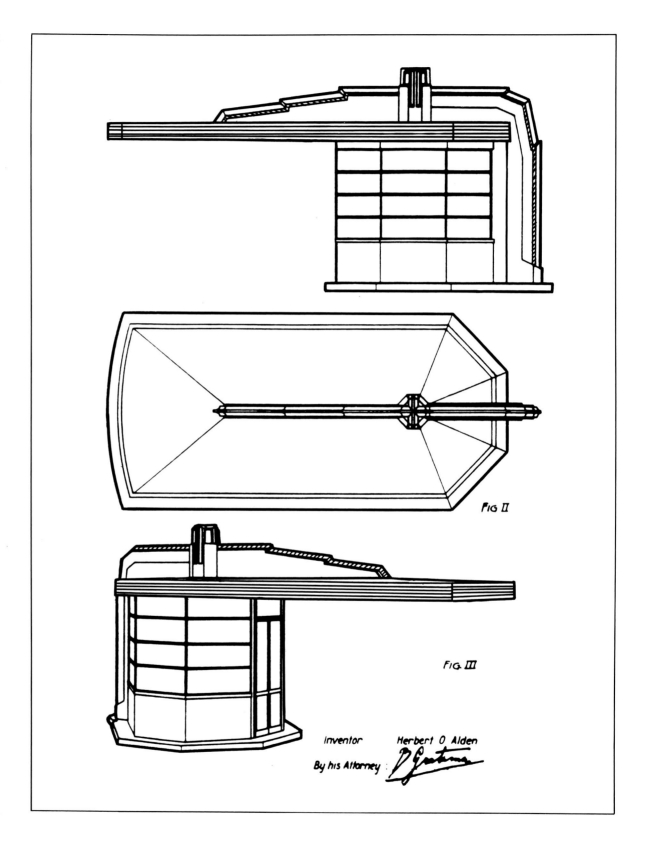

that "every man who plans the shape and line and color of an object—whether it is a painting, statue, chair, sewing machine, house, bridge, or locomotive—is an artist," Teague came well suited for the job. Texaco had secured not only a talented designer but a sensitive artist uniquely in tune with the needs of the public, at the same time completely aware of the most pleasing in machine aesthetics.

But Teague considered more than just his own likes and dislikes in formulating the new station designs. A cross section of consumer and dealer reactions compiled from a twenty-station survey yielded basic requirements that would

Ramseier's Texaco Station

Ed Ramseier and his classic Texaco Service station located off US 36 in Idalia, Colorado. Built from the ground up with his own hands, his Texaco station provided gasoline, service, and parts to countless motorists making their way across the country. With his friendly attitude and eye-catching house style building, it was easy to pull 'em in. Larry Shirkey

Service was the essence of his place. You could see the pride by checking out one of the super-clean restrooms or by observing his attitude as he wiped windows and checked oil.

The route of US 36 cuts a solitary path of crackling blacktop straight through northeast Colorado and beyond. Its two-lane ribbon brazenly shoots through rustic towns with names like Strasburg, Lindon, Cope, Joes and Last Chance. Vast oceans of farmland undulate with life on both sides of the thoroughfare, in synch with the breeze. As the mile markers click past, a nostalgic blend of people and places foresaken by time unfolds in the images rushing by. This is the real American road.

Twelve miles before crossing the Kansas border and 2½ road hours from Denver, a special remnant of roadside history lies dormant just outside the small community of Idalia.

Like a dusty time machine tucked away on the roadside, a once beautiful Texaco station stands in helpless decay. Distinguished from the landscape, the white brick walls and red roof of the small building grab your attention from the repetitive roadway. Standing like totems, silver and red gas pumps complete the scene.

As you pull off the road to take a closer look, the mirage deteriorates to one of peeling paint and disrepair. The globes that once graced the top of the fifties-style pumps are gone. Only the glass Sky-Chief and Ethyl placards remain. Faded paint and torn-up nail holes highlight the spots where signs and fixtures once were. The uncanny feeling of an ominous presence dominates the site. Like a ghost town, the scene is strangely deserted. If you listen closely, you can almost hear the faint call of "Fill 'er up" riding piggyback on the whistling wind. Nearby, dust devils whip up whirlwinds of debris in ironic agreement with the vacant desolation.

It's hard to believe that only ten years ago this forsaken outpost was a shining example of the classic roadside refueling stop. Back then, it was a local attraction and tourist stop, admired by thousands of highway travelers heading across the country. Ed Ramseier made sure of that.

It was Ed's idea to open the station, taking valuable experience from a farm implement dealership and garage he operated through the Second World War. Calling on his inborn heritage for Swiss artisanship and utilizing his blacksmithing skills, he constructed it from scratch. His picturesque gas station was completed in 1950, a new decade marking the birth of an important refueling stop in rural Colorado.

Operating like the inner workings of a fine clock, Ramseier's Texaco serviced cars and pumped gasoline for many years. The motoring public enjoyed stopping to partake of its homespun utility. All the wayfaring souls of the endless American road trip were Ed's special audience, his people.

Hanging on the walls or sitting on a shelf, every imaginable part and gadget filled the tiny station building. Points and plugs for a 1958 Fairlane? No problem—you could get them down at Ramseier's! Ed stocked the important items travelers needed and enjoyed providing a service. Having the parts to keep road vehicles mobile was his reason for being,

his life. It all mattered to him, even the smallest detail.

Suddenly, unforeseen events in the world marketplace endangered Ed's livelihood and business in 1973. The specter of the OPEC oil embargo had threatened the gas supply, causing thousands of marginally profitable stations to be abandoned. Independent operators like Ed were badly burned. Without warning, the nature of the small-town service station had changed, forever altering the visage of the road.

Now, the remnants of Ed's picture-perfect gasoline station persist as proud reminders of a service value that once permeated American society. Every piece of broken pump, crumbling brick and fragment of metal is an embodiment of those virtues. Once the tools Ed used to weave his personal brand of roadside magic, the decaying building and rusting pumps left behind are more than special. He breathed life into them all and empowered them with the personality that made them great.

For Ed, it was a reality few people could hope for. He made Ramseier's what it was—complete with its full service, clean restrooms, and friendly attitude. To the seasoned roadside traveler addicted to the drone of four wheels at fifty-five miles per hour, the passing of Ed and his old-fashioned gas station is like the loss of an old friend.

Ed enjoyed having the parts people needed and stocked a wide variety of automotive merchandise in his small station building. When a car pulled in for service, he almost always had the parts required to repair it.

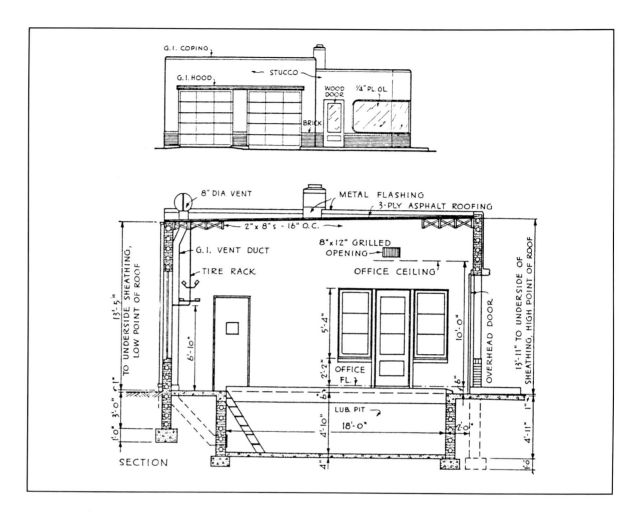

determine the attributes of the new designs, which were fed into the design equation. Certain needs such as well-lit and efficient service bays, proper restroom space, ample sales areas, good lighting and image standardization by use of color schemes were universal desires. In addition, the new stations had to look modern and efficient, as well as provide for a "concentration of sales appeal" at the pump.

To do that, unnecessary architectural details were stripped away, the common denominator of "purpose" dictating design. Partly influenced by the unadorned simplicity of the International Style, Teague presented a number of distinct models to the board of directors by 1937.

By use of rounded rooflines and aerodynamic gas pumps mounted on smoothed islands in the drive-through, the new structures contained marked references to the Streamline Moderne style. Three streamlining pinstripes running horizontally across the parapet reinforced the look, implying a renewed sense of speed and efficiency for the motorist. Exterior surfaces paneled in porcelain-enameled steel were accentuated by the strategic arrangement of red Texaco "stars" constructed in multifaceted relief. Optional canopies characterized by two curved fins extended out from below the roofline as a continuation of the racy green speed lines.

For the display of products, a group of large glass windows occupied one quarter of the frontal perimeter. Located at the center of these paned view-ports, a "look-through" door leading to the office sported the proprietor's name

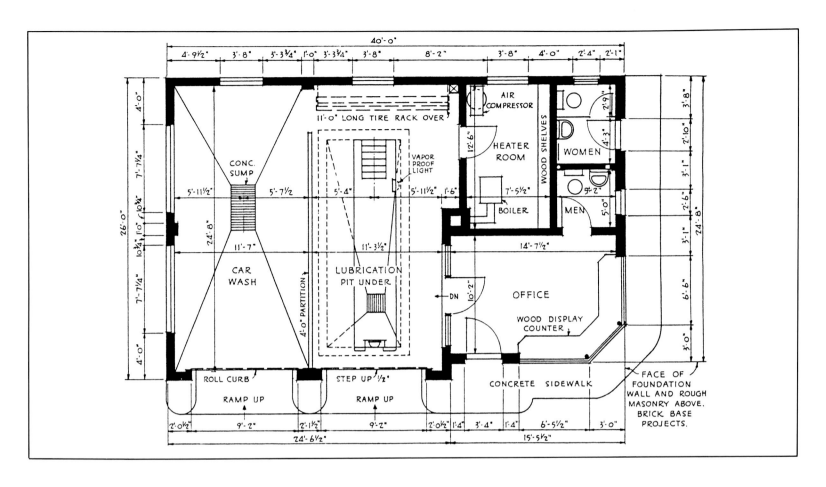

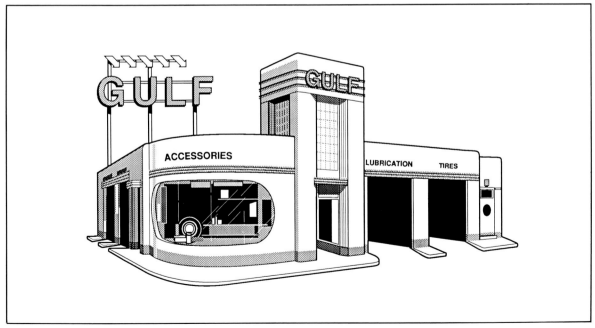

Station plans for Standard Oil Company of New Jersey box-type service stations from the *1944 Architectural Record.* Standard Oil Company

Every company had its version of the thirties box, including Gulf Oil Company. The stylings of Streamline Moderne influenced their design extensively, with a large rounded sales window, a porthole restroom window, a center pylon adorned in flow-line neon and ubiquitous speed lines running across the parapet. *Gabriele Witzel*

Type C–36 One-Car Gable Roof Lubritory Station designed by the firm of Frederick G. Frost, Jr. Still reluctant to go all the way with the box style, Standard Oil Company of New York built a number of these colonialized stations on the East Coast to complement the region's architecture. *1938 rendering by Donald Dodge, courtesy Frederick G. Frost, Jr.*

Next page
Type I–36 Corner Bay Station for Standard Oil Company of New York. By the end of the thirties, the domestic imagery of Socony's station buildings was slowly being replaced by more modern designs. In this precursor to the "drum" design of 1940, the decorative pediment was finally dropped as visual references to the house were eliminated. *1939 rendering by Donald Dodge, courtesy Frederick G. Frost, Jr.*

affixed in red sans serif lettering above the overhead buttress. Individual service bays were also identified with lettering pertaining to their particular function, whether it be Marfak lubrication, washing or other services. With garage bay doors echoing the cubed panels of the porcelain exterior, the entire station layout communicated a new dynamic symmetry.

By 1940, more than 500 of Texaco's stations were built or revamped to Teague's specifications. With all the precision of a modern machine, the gleaming white streamlined box was soon to become the newly exalted form of gasoline station architecture. The house as sacrosanct identity for the basic American refueling business had seen the end of its days.

With all cosmetic disguises lifted, the roadside building that had gasoline pumps installed in front now appeared to be exactly what it was—and always should have been: not a Grecian monument or Chinese pagoda or country cottage, but simply a refueling station where the motorist could purchase combustible fluid.

Those Slye Computers

Bob Jauch, chief engineer for the Wayne Oil Tank & Pump Company, decided to visit the manufacturing facilities of a Hartford-based firm known as the Veeder-Root Company in 1932. He had a close friendship with Walter Merz, a sales representative with the original Root Company before it merged with Veeder, and desired

to tour the new company's expanded facilities. After several days of just quietly looking over the plant, Jauch met with company officials and disclosed Wayne's goal to develop a new type of computer metering device for gasoline pumps. Veeder-Root appeared to be the likely candidate to help build it.

After analyzing Jauch's variator prototype, Ed Slye, a skilled engineer working for Veeder-Root, said it was "nothing more than a gear box" and that he could design one that was simpler, more economical and able to perform better functionally. A stunned Jauch quickly withdrew and consulted with Wayne's president, Bill Griffin, who countered with a statement implying that the Wayne company should be entitled to any improvements Veeder-Root might make on its original designs.

The familiar Texaco star mounted on a stylish pole was part of architect Walter Dorwin Teague's station redesign effort in the late thirties. All over America, the same round placard would be erected to standardize the Texas Company's look and bolster its image with the motoring public.

Early logo from Veeder-Root Company, manufacturer of the Slye computer that revolutionized the design of gas pumps and the way gasoline was sold in the mid-thirties. *Veeder-Root*

Typical Socony products and service station attendant's hat.

During World War II, most of the male work force was overseas fighting for the cause. Meanwhile, back home, women of all ages were being recruited to do their share by operating the pumps at the neighborhood service station. *Atlantic Richfield Company*

Once legal matters were put into order, gearing wizard Slye began his work. Within a short time, Veeder-Root had what it called its new eight-inch computer. Because of Jauch's preliminary work on the device, the Slye patent for the new computing device was eventually assigned to Wayne.

At the time, Wayne was the only gas pump manufacturer to implement the new device and Veeder-Root's only customer for the new computer. Marketing met strong resistance when it solicited the other pump companies to switch over from the outmoded dial-face designs to the more accurate mechanical calculator. The large oil companies feigned disinterest too, well aware that Veeder-Root's new measuring instrument rendered obsolete all the pumping equipment currently in operation. Because none of the competition had a product that could compare with the new eight-inch computer gas pumps, negative reactions prevailed.

Regardless of the initial acceptance the advanced pumps received, Wayne knew it had a

winner and concentrated on selling the pumps to independent service station owners and small oil companies. Panel trucks toured the country, complete with a fully assembled gasoline pump mounted in the rear for demonstration purposes. Independents liked what they saw, and soon orders began to pile up for the highly accurate pumps.

Like kids in a candy store, station lessees under the jurisdiction of the major oil companies wondered why they had to use outdated machinery and demanded that the parent companies purchase the new units. Bowing to operator pressure, the remaining pump manufacturers fell into place and were licensed to integrate the new computer variator into their models. Eventually, the entire field of twelve pump manufacturers had signed royalty agreements. Those that didn't and used similar designs were soon seen in court.

With a "head for figures" (as touted in one of Veeder-Root's later slogans for the pump), the new computer calculator proved to be a major improvement in the development of the gasoline pump. Instantly, it changed the way motor fuel was sold, wherever it was installed. Now, instead of reading a dial-face gallon indicator and having to consult a corresponding price chart for the final cash total, a station attendant could simply glance at the computer numbers for the calculated price after pumping gasoline. Automatically, myriad tiny gears and wheels spinning inside the gas pump housing totaled the figures. A renewed customer confidence bloomed, as the chance for operator error and dishonesty had been eliminated.

Gasoline stations didn't have to resort to using underhanded tricks to increase profits, though. All they had to do was buy the new pumps, install them and let the spinning numbers of the computer calculator work their magic. At the time, using a conventional gas pump meant for instance giving back twenty cents to a customer requesting a five-gallon gasup (worth ninety cents) and paying with a $1 bill. Using the new computers, the sales approach of the attendant could be changed to a question: "One dollar's worth, or two dollars' worth?" In either case, operators would pick up practically

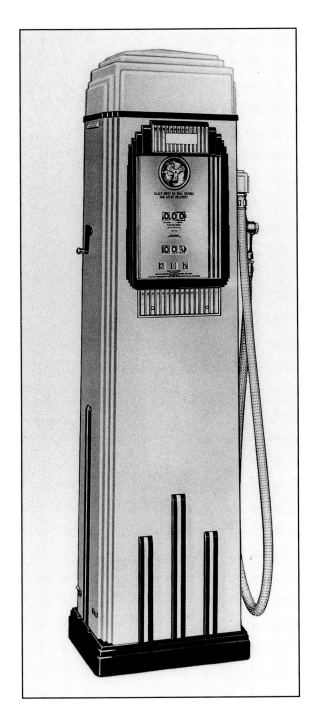

The Tokheim Moneymaker 36B gasoline pump was one of the first new gasoline pumps to use the new numeric computer introduced by Veeder-Root Company in 1933. Complete with glass dome and chrome embellishments rivaling those on the latest automotive models, this 1937 gas pump offered a level of prosperity to station owners eager to pull themselves out of the Depression-era slump. With the ability to sell gasoline by dollars instead of gallons, the new units played a large part in increasing the average sale. *Tokheim Corporation*

Refinery-sealed oil cans did not come into general use at America's gasoline stations until the mid-thirties. Kendall Oil experimented with their use around 1934, and glass oil dispensers were soon replaced. By the fifties, when this photo was taken, Golden Shell Motor Oil housed in the handy throwaway canister could be purchased at the neighborhood service station.

Machine Age Gas Pumps

During the late twenties, the architectural machine known as the skyscraper made its monolithic debut in metropolitan areas throughout the country. The new setback building structures boasted large bases and ascending levels that became increasingly smaller; made of steel, stone and glass, they were popping up across the country.

The silhouette of the city was undergoing a dramatic change, influencing the outward appearance of the gasoline station fuel pump right along with it. The cylindrical designs of the visible-register and clock-face pumps were being modified to evoke the angular geometrics of their larger counterparts. Updated gasoline pumps mirrored their form in miniature, including details indicative of their modern architecture. Displaying uncanny similarities, advertising played on the trend and featured pumps set against a backdrop of modern buildings in publications like *Super Service Station*.

an eleven percent increase in their gallonage sold. Because of this new way of looking at purchasing gasoline, the attendant could sell on the basis of "Shall I fill 'er up?" for the first time in gasoline pumping history.

Texaco magazine advertisement from 1934 featuring Texaco comedian Ed Wynn and his own special brand of humor. *Texaco Inc.*

WAIT!
DON'T SHOOT
YOUR CAR DEALER

Phillips 66 Poly Gas
will <u>start</u> that cold motor!

POLYMERIZED

Phillips 66

If your temper flares up and boils over because your cold motor won't start, don't blame your car.

Any engine in good mechanical condition *will start* provided that the gasoline in the tank is "hot" enough. And almost any good mechanic will tell you that *high test* Phillips 66 Poly Gas is "hotter'n a firecracker!"

Why? Because Phillips is the WORLD'S LARGEST PRODUCER of *natural* high test gasoline and offers extra high test without a penny of extra price. So try a tankful of this energy-packed, POLYmerized, custom-tailored gasoline.

You tip-toe the button, and there is no missing . . . sputtering . . . or backfiring. What a kick! when your motor rolls over with no gnashing of teeth, purr-r-r-s into instant action, warms up fast. Besides, you save the miles usually wasted by excessive use of the choke with ordinary low-test fuels.

Your first set-to with a cold, balky motor will probably send you searching for a Phillips Gas Station . . . But why wait until you have starting trouble? Start enjoying faster starting tomorrow morning by getting Phillips 66 Poly Gas tonight . . . at any Orange and Black 66 Shield.

Phill-up with Phillips for *Instant Starting*

"Wait! Don't Shoot Your Car Dealer." Circa 1937 advertisement for Phillips Petroleum Company's new Poly-gas instant-starting motor fuel. *Courtesy Phillips Petroleum Company*

"Fuel of the Future" today
SHELL GASOLINE

DON'T think of Shell Gasoline as a tankful of uninteresting liquid —you can't see the molecules, but your engine feels their dynamic power!

A scientific advance has raised its Road Performance Rating (RPR) to an all-time high . . .

THERMAL CONVERSION makes it extra rich in *iso*-compounds similar to *iso-octane*— first produced commercially by Shell scientists to give America 100-octane

aviation gasoline . . . fuel so powerful and efficient that it led to an increase in the speed and flying range of America's planes up to 30%!

This scientific advance saves on the costliest driving you do—Stop-and-Go. And increased RPR means increased responsiveness—puts a new thrill in your motoring! Get high RPR Shell Gasoline (at regular price) or Shell Premium at your neighborhood Shell dealer's. Try a tankful today.

AUGUST SERVICE TIP

"Thoro-Fast" service means quick but careful—that's my free-service pledge! Your car needs a "Thoro-Fast" check-up every hundred miles.

The forties brought new advancements in gasoline, and Shell Oil Company promoted its "fuel of the future" by placing a number of advertisements in national magazines. With smiling service attendant and shell-topped gas pump, a free service tip was offered up for consumption. The emphasis was still on service, with the image of a "real person" the central theme of the advertisement.

"Metropolitanism" drastically changed the appearance of the urban office tower and steered the design directions of the gasoline pump toward a bold new course. Taking cues from automotive-influenced designs like the Chrysler Building in New York City, pump manufacturers readily incorporated the architectural features of Art Deco into many of their new creations.

Appearing above the computer face, small triangular windows arranged in radiating semicircles set the foundation for many pump motifs by the late thirties. Chrome-plated escutcheons and multiple-ridged embellishments echoed the latest automotive trim installed on car models. A variety of decorative forms were soon competing for attention on the exterior of the modern gas pump, including wide vertical pin-stripes. Curved support wings and rounded cabinet tops came into fashion with a number of manufacturers and were integrated into the most current models. Thin decorative strips accented the sides of some pumps, running from top to bottom at the corners.

Distinctive speed lines borrowed from German architect Erich Mendelsohn's visionary sketches found their way into the styling of units like the Tokheim Moneymaker 36B. Arranged in vertical rows originating from the center of the pump base, these three polished accents allowed the motorist a preview of the machine age streamlining soon to dominate all manner of building, machinery and conveyance.

The smoothing characteristics of streamlining began to hone away the sharp edges of the American gas pump by 1939 as many industrial

By the early forties, the uniform of the Gulf station attendant was upgraded to reflect new styles of fashion. Baggy breeches were replaced by simple straight-leg pants and restrictive waist-jackets eliminated for comfortable work shirts. The military salute was toned down to a personal wave as shoes became more stylish. The bow tie and cap remained, along with the friendliness and helpful demeanor the public had grown accustomed to. *Chevron Corporation*

Standard Oil sold automotive lubricants under the RPM Supreme label and offered free lens tissue in the shape of an oil can to the customer.

designers influenced by the contoured bodies and parabolic tails of aircraft like the Douglas DC-3 applied the look of curved surfaces to their latest projects.

As the hard lines of the setback idiom began to soften, a more purified style of machine aesthetics was coming into vogue. A new "prime object" had been born, and the race to repackage common household articles and consumer products was on. Decorative details were dropped as the modernistic influences of Art Deco were replaced by more unified designs.

With the Depression making a financial impact on profits, manufacturers were eager to redesign everything from implements to appliances, improving functionality while incor-

porating a totally modern look. Advances in metalworking technology and the die-pressing machinery that made the new forms possible had finally been perfected. Now, electric refrigerators were made more aerodynamic, vacuum cleaners swifter looking and gasoline pumps streamlined with contoured cowlings covering mechanical components. Only a chrome-flanged window and glass spinner gauge identified the gasoline pump for what it was. The aesthetic influences of the machine age had transformed it into a minimalist box—one that conveyed the static illusion of efficiency and speed to the passing motorist.

The Tokheim Moneymaker 36B gasoline pump complete with jumbo sales case with locking hinged door was ideal for the display of motor oils, fan belts, spark plugs, windshield wipers, headlamps and other accessories. The new display case models facilitated easy sales at the pump and generated the eye appeal required to move new levels of merchandise at the service station. The gas pump was now more than a machine; it was also an integral part of station display and marketing. *Tokheim Corporation*

Next page
In the thirties, this demonstration laboratory on wheels toured the Phillips Petroleum Company's sales territory to inform customers about—and sell them on—the technical characteristics of its new gasolines. By selective blending, Phillips' scientists perfected "controlled volatility" motor fuels. This meant simply that the volatility was controlled for climate: the fuels were more volatile in cold weather, less so in hot weather. *Courtesy Phillips Petroleum Company*

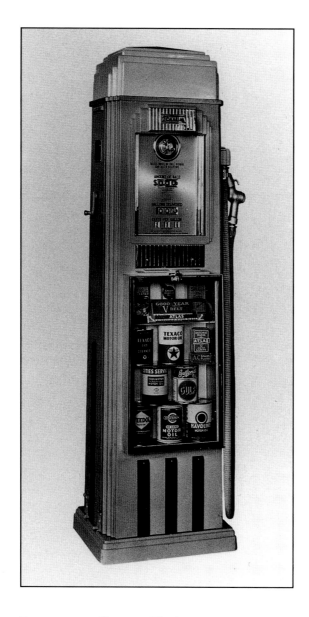

Restrooms: Fact or Fiction?

Until the late thirties, the gasoline station held a bad reputation when it came to the "unmentionable" needs of motorists and their families. Finding a roadside privy with all the comforts of home during the Depression years was highly unlikely. The lackadaisical maintenance and housekeeping habits practiced by busy station personnel often left washrooms dirty, unsanitary and for the most part unattractive. Consequently, the gasoline station restroom was used only when absolutely necessary.

A handful of thoughtful stations tried to establish the notion of pristine facilities early on, but the "movement" never really caught on, relegating the gas station washroom to a status of low priority. The Western Oil Refinery Company experimented with a beautiful carpeted lounge complete with wicker accessories as part of its ladies room at one of its first California stations in the early twenties, but it was one of the few exceptions. Whether situated on Main Street or on the local highway, the filling station restroom was a room one didn't prefer to "rest" in for very long.

Selling gasoline and ensuring that the mechanical systems of an automobile were running at top form were not conducive to good house-keeping habits, as mechanics and customers usually had to use the same toilet facilities. With the pumping of gas, airing up of tires, cleaning of windshields and many other dirty tasks that had to be taken care of under the hood, keeping a bathroom clean for the needs of traveling motorists was too much to ask of the average station attendant. Grease-stained hands didn't make the job any easier, either. In the days before equality of the sexes, a mechanic handy with a grease gun and torque wrench often did a sorry piece of work when it came to scrubbing a floor.

Luckily for the motorist, a welcome turn of events came about in the late thirties when a handful of the major oil companies decided to take stock of their stations' shortcomings and upgrade their washroom facilities. As a way to increase patronage and elevate their status in an area that had largely been ignored by many of their competitors, they improved conditions and put facilities in good working order. An extensive campaign of public promotion was implemented to inform the gasoline purchaser of the new changes, and by the end of the thirties, the degraded image of the gas station lounge was well on its way to improvement.

Riders of the White Patrol

Texaco was the first major oil company to pioneer the development and marketing of clean service station facilities to a receptive public. Beginning in 1938, its registered restrooms appeared by the thousands at gasoline stations

105

Texaco magazine advertisement from 1941. Like the mailcarrier, gas station attendants were ready in rain, sleet or snow. *Texaco Inc.*

ALL NIGHT LONG... *You're Welcome*

Remember that late drive home in a blinding rain, with the gas gauge creeping toward "empty"? Remember how one service station after another was blacked-out, closed? Remember worrying about the long, wet walk home?

★　　★　　★

But that needn't happen to you this summer. Once more Texaco Dealers have pioneered! They now offer you all-night-service on every main highway in America throughout the summer touring season.

No matter how late the hour or how bad the night...a Texaco Dealer is ready to supply you with either of those two famous Texaco

Gasolines, *Fire-Chief* or *SKY CHIEF*. He will give your motor needed protection with *Insulated* Havoline, or Texaco Motor Oil. He will clean that rain-blurred windshield, offer you the shelter and convenience of his *Registered* Rest Room, send you safely on your way. Yes! Day or night... *You're Welcome* AT

TEXACO DEALERS

TUNE IN : "Millions for Defense" All Star Radio Program every Wednesday Night—Columbia Broadcasting System—9:00 E.D.T., 8:00 E.S.T., 8:00 C.D.T., 7:00 C.S.T., 6:00 M.S.T., 5:00 P.S.T.

Posing for a picture with Chairman Frank Phillips, members of the elite Highway Hostesses prepare to venture forth on their appointed rounds. An integral part of Phillips "Certified Restroom" campaign initially begun in 1939, this courageous group of registered nurses was responsible for making sure that gas station washrooms were well cleaned and stocked—always ready for the motorist who wished to use them. Canvassing the countryside in cream-colored automobiles to personally validate the status of Phillips service station washrooms, their visits could come at any time of day or night.
Courtesy Phillips Petroleum Company

all across the country. With cleanliness guaranteed, each unit was registered by the company for the customer's protection and was individually numbered. Touting these facilities as A Texaco Dealer Service were friendly green and white signs positioned beneath the tapered Texaco pole curbside where all passing traffic could readily see.

Behind two doors labeled with green and white placards signifying cubicles for men and ladies were public restrooms like no others. The beautifully tiled interiors of the new Teague station designs sparkled with an unprecedented cleanliness. Modern, well-maintained toilet equipment matched gleaming white sinks that boasted hot and cold running water. Fully equipped with fresh soap to clean hands and a towel to dry them, the registered units promised a level of comfort never before seen at the typical gas outlet. Women could now freshen up without embarrassment and children could be allowed to use the facilities without worry.

To make sure that the new washrooms lived up to their immaculate image and that the station owners were doing their part, Texaco maintained a fleet of White Patrol Chevrolets to police company dealers. Trained inspectors roamed about in all-white Master DeLuxe Sport Coupes identified by the familiar Texaco insignia, cruising the highways and byways solely for the purpose of restroom inspection. Their mission: Seek out any dirt and grime that might

threaten to sully the newly upgraded image of the company's ceramic-tiled water closets so enthusiastically applauded by the public.

All forty-eight states fell under the white-glove scrutiny of the group's dedicated servants. Not one speck of dirt would be allowed to go unbroomed by the dauntless crusaders of the White Patrol. Dispatched on their mission in the dark of night, dead of winter or heat of summer, they would ride the highways as unsung heroes of the American motorist, keeping the institution of the free and clean service station restroom an amenity the automobile owner could rely on 365 days a year. It was more than just a job, it was the patrol's duty to all motorists—one that would ensure that every registered restroom lived up to its neat and tidy billing:

"Whether you're a little "tourist," or a grown-up tourist there are times when nothing is so welcome as the familiar green and white sign of a Texaco Registered Rest Room. You can trust that sign. You know that it means, "Here is a restroom scrupulously neat. A restroom equipped with running water, towels and all the necessities for comfort and cleanliness." Back of that spic-and-span cleanliness is the Texaco dealer's pledge. And back of that pledge is the watchfulness of the "White Patrol" . . . inspection cars that constantly check each of the Registered Rest Rooms."

Legend of the Highway Hostess

Enlisting a crew of attractive young women qualified as registered nurses, Phillips Petroleum

Mobil magazine advertisement from 1942. The headline "Protect Horsepower" was ironic, as the horseless carriage was putting both the horse and the blacksmith out of work.

109

Company unveiled its own campaign to clean up the service station restroom in the summer of 1939. Calling for the in-person validation of each of its new "Certified" restrooms throughout the Phillips sales territory, the company dispatched six enrollees in this trained medical group in personalized vehicles to investigate station facilities at random. As unique members of an elite inspection team, the Highway Hostesses were responsible for making sure that gas station washrooms were not only well cleaned and stocked but always ready for the motorist who wished to use them.

Doubling as ambassadors for the company, the Highway Hostesses "helped to sell Phillips 66 by their courteous manner, pleasant personalities, and willingness to aid anyone in distress." Cheerfully, they directed tourists to suitable restaurants, hotels and scenic attractions, as well as took the time to discuss infant hygiene with traveling mothers.

Dressed in light blue uniforms and military-style caps, they reminded one of recruits for the Women's Air Corps. Their white shoes, stockings and vest pocket handkerchiefs also conjured up images of the local waitress who poured coffee at the neighborhood pancake house. A Phillips 66 insignia patch completed their ensemble. Any motorist who spied them canvassing the countryside in cream-colored automobiles sporting green fenders knew exactly which company and restroom they represented.

The group proved their usefulness to Phillips and a skeptical public as more than just restroom checkers only months after the program started. Encountering an automobile accident while traveling through the company's Kansas City marketing region, the team was called upon to assist five members of a professional baseball team injured when their car accidentally rolled over. At the scene, the well-trained hostesses calmly administered first aid and spread good cheer with unflinching poise. The Phillips promotion department would have been proud. If an award were ever given for a motorized group of Florence Nightingales, the Phillips 66 Highway Hostesses would have received top honors.

Twin Tokheim pumps with "spinners" at the R. F. Waters Feed Store in Dumfries, Virginia, converted to offer lead-free Texaco gasoline in the seventies.

As word of the Texaco Registered Rest Rooms and Phillips Certified restrooms spread, other oil companies soon joined the cleanup parade and implemented their version of the service station bathroom. For a brief moment in the time line of the American gas station, the motorist who desired pleasant facilities for personal comfort could stop at almost any gasoline business and be treated to clean surroundings.

Within a few years, however, the race for restroom cleanliness inexplicably died out. Without fanfare, the frenzy of registration and certification mysteriously ended as signs were quietly removed. Inspecting nurses were discharged of their duties or reassigned as the White Patrol vehicles were permanently parked. Uniforms and company caps were put into mothballs until no traces of the guaranteed restroom phenomenon remained. Public conveniences at gas stations all across the nation slowly reverted back to their previous status. Soon, the reign of the Highway Hostesses and Texaco inspectors was a distant memory, the transitory appearance of the clean gas station restroom only a dream.

Chapter 6

Metamorphosis of an American Icon, 1947–1992

Just when it began to appear that the American service station had found its architectural niche, a new wrinkle in the marketing of gasoline developed. George Urich, a California independent dealer, dreamed up a revolutionary new station concept targeted for California, in which customers could pump their own gas—pocketing a nice savings in the process. Initially opening three of his outlets in the Los Angeles area in 1947 with two competitors following, he forever altered the nature of the gasoline station and inadvertently set into motion a gas marketing controversy that would rage for years.

Urich's new Gas-A-Terias consisted of eighteen to twenty-one gasoline pumps set on islands lined up at right angles to the street. Cars drove up to any one of these gas dispensers in two long rows to refuel and were sometimes parked twelve or fourteen abreast during peak periods. Urich claimed that as little as 2½ minutes was required to pump one's own gas, giving motorists the ability to get in and out fast.

A New Age of Self-Service

Station attendants once eager to check the oil and wipe the windows were eliminated in the interest of reducing the expense of salaries. A bevy of six girls in tight sweaters and slacks replaced them, racing around the surfaced lot in roller skates much like their satin-costumed counterparts working the neighborhood hamburger joint. Gliding from island to island, they collected money and made change amidst a mad frenzy of vehicles and whirring gas pumps.

Courtesy services were relegated to a separate portion of the lot. After gasoline was pumped and the cashier was paid, customers helped themselves to water or air. In a small booth located at the center of all this activity, a supervisor watched the proceedings through glass windows. A public-address system allowed customers to be reprimanded over an external speaker if seen smoking or doing something inappropriate.

For the customer in search of a bargain, all this unaided service saved a considerable amount of money. Large storage tanks with the capability to take on a fuel truck's entire tank-load added to this retail discount, enabling the self-service station to price its gasoline lower and pass the value on to the motorist. The unbranded gasolines sold were at least five cents per gallon cheaper than gasolines at any major conventional station. For the average citizen just trying to make a living in postwar America, it wasn't hard to calculate that enough change to buy two loaves of bread could routinely be saved, just by filling up the tank themselves.

Open twenty-four hours a day, some self-service stations in southern California averaged sales of close to 100,000 gallons per month. Compared with the 10,000 to 20,000 gallons

Sunset on the glory days of the American gas station. The Pegasus flies above the roof of Gordon W. Smith's Mobil station in Eden Prairie, Minnesota, one of the last neon Flying Horses in service anywhere in the United States in this age of remodeled modern gas stations. Ironically, Smith's station has been redecorated several times over the years and now toes the line with the corporate image, but the Pegasus has remained as a blazing neon beacon through all of the changes. *Michael Dregni*

The OPEC oil embargo began the decline of the small-time, mom-and-pop gas station and the beginnings of the corporate superstation. This station runs lights up the Texas night. The times, they are a changin'.

115

Slim Olsen's large-volume forty-three-pump "world's largest" self-service station served a lot of highway customers in the mid-fifties. By use of a large sign dwarfing the station hut, the motorist could make no mistake as to the nature of the business being advertised and where to pull off the roadway. It was all just part of attracting the valued customer. *National Archives*

per month pumped at conventional gas stations, this was a large volume of fuel. Able to handle 2,000 to 3,000 cars per day, the new self-service stations did a landmark business around the clock.

The oil companies looked favorably toward this ability to move large quantities of distillate and secretly encouraged the self-service establishments. It was a tough position for them to take, though. They didn't want to stand in the way of lower gasoline prices for the consumer and were worried about alienating owners of conventional stations who were being hurt by the discount prices. Because of heavy investment in existing station designs and uncertainty about the effect construction of self-service stations would have on them, the major oil refiners decided to stay away from opening company-owned self-service outlets, for the time being. For now, it would be a game for the independents—one that would soon force many conventional stations to go bankrupt.

Casting the First Stone

Labeling the opening of the Gas-A-Teria as nothing more than a "strictly local phenomenon," *Business Week* played down the self-service openings as just another California fad. Others whose livelihood suffered perceived the incursion as more serious and took matters into their own hands.

A barrage of telephone calls against the new refueling method were fielded by a surprised Urich almost immediately after he opened his first two stations. Anonymous letters calling for his ouster poured in, containing a variety of threats. Two of the male relief workers who replaced the female cashiers during the night shift were beaten up by a group of thugs. An operator who opened the first self-service outlet in Hackensack, New Jersey, was welcomed into business by the delivery of rocks through his windows. The self-service station had gotten off to a controversial beginning. A gasoline station where customers served themselves was a new threat quickly eroding the profits of established gas stations not inclined to change their modes of operation.

116

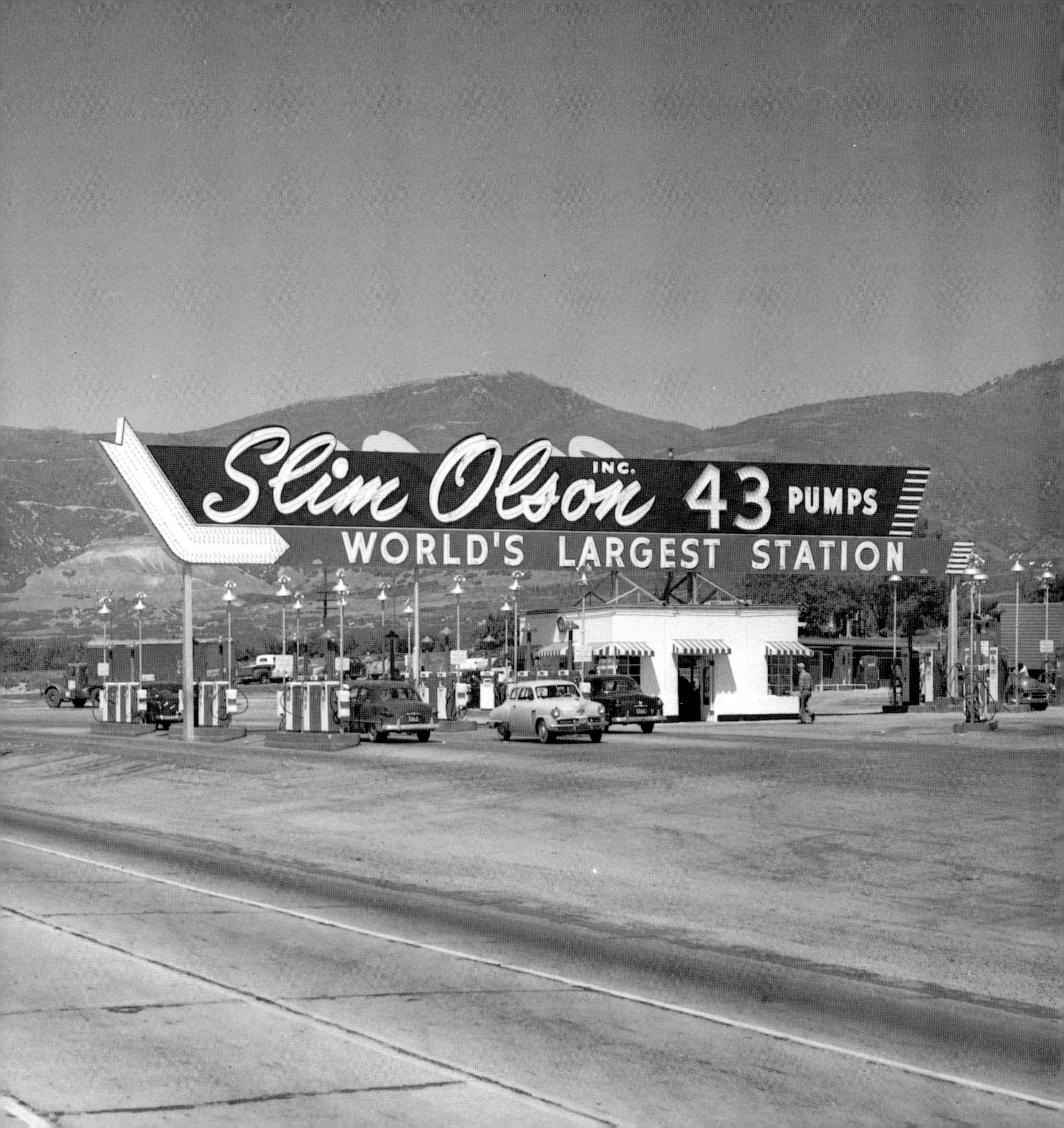
Slim Olson INC.
43 PUMPS
WORLD'S LARGEST STATION

This unusual iceberg gas station located on US Route 66 in Albuquerque, New Mexico, used visual games to attract vehicles in 1948. Sometimes, the small independent operator had to rely on architectural theatrics to draw in the business. *National Archives*

A less violent campaign of commercial warfare quickly mounted as 250,000 well-organized conventional gas station operators stood united against the self-serve businesses. Successful in exerting political force nationwide, the group soon had the self-service gas station outlawed in ten states, with seven more states considering similar bills.

Detractors of the self-serve methodology pointed to the lack of safety at the controversial outlets and cited the possibility of increased danger from fire. The cries proved moot, however; with more than twenty-seven stations operating in the Los Angeles area, not one call was ever received by local fire departments. In further support, a survey conducted by the *National Petroleum News* reported that in a typical city with at least thirty-five self-serve stations, less fuel leakage and better housekeeping were found in most of the outlets. Also, the National Fire Protection Association found the safety of new gas businesses equal to that of conventional stations. As long as customers were diligently monitored for the use of improper containers, smoking or the inability to pump their own gas, safety problems could be headed off before trouble began.

Without enough real evidence against the self-service gasoline station and with no valid reasons for discontinuing its operation, the oppo-

sition group lost strength as fast as it had gained it. Self-serve-style gasoline pumping was here to stay. The conventional gas station had to change with the times and give the public what it wanted, or find some other way to compete in the gasoline marketplace.

After all, the motoring public liked the savings realized at the self-service pump. Who could blame them? From their short viewpoint on the roadway, it was hard to see that their newfound exuberance for the Gas-A-Teria would eventually eliminate more than just high prices.

Airplanes and Icebergs

As early as the thirties, independent operators strove to make their establishments stand out from the crowd. Without the years of adver-

tising and image building that the major oil companies had, they faced a public unfamiliar with their private brands. To survive, the small chains and family operations had to be more innovative in the design of their stations and the methods they used to market gasoline. While the oblong box design was profitable for the majors, elaborate roadside architecture calculated to attract attention promised to bring more customers into stations lacking a national image.

A number of attention-getting designs were built, employing a diverse range of architectural theatrics with larger-than-life gimmicks as the centerpiece. One gasoline station in Portland, Oregon, had a B-17 Flying Fortress bomber mounted on the roof, its imposing wings adorned in bright neon. The station's enterprising owner,

The Bomber Gas, Art Lacey's service station in Portland, Oregon. Lacey bought the B-17 Flying Fortress from the US government as war surplus in 1947 for $1,500. He flew the plane north and mounted it atop his station to attract passersby. The bomber has remained in place while over the years the gas pumps have changed and the station house has been remodelled. A great way of life. *Milo Peltzer via Scott Thompson*

119

Once the curbside gasoline pump was outlawed from the city streets of America, it survived only in rural areas. This is the general store and post office for Goldvein, Virginia, along Route 17 in 1942. *National Archives*

Next page
By the forties, the architectural firm of Frederick G. Frost, Jr., was given the go-ahead to design a modern station unit for Standard Oil Company of New York's new service outlets. Influenced by the cylindrical nature of an oil can, the drum design, clad in gleaming white porcelain-enameled steel, was built in many locations across the country, including this one in Philadelphia. With its oversized plate glass windows and transparent service bay doors, it became the perfect showcase for Socony-Vacuum's extensive product line of tires, batteries and accessories. *Courtesy Mobil Corporation*

Art Lacey, picked up the secondhand aircraft for $1,500 and flew it to Portland himself for the installation.

Another independent operator with a penchant for the unusual constructed his station building to resemble a large iceberg, right in the middle of New Mexico. An environmental rarity in that arid part of the country, it easily received the attention anticipated from passing motorists. A sparse gathering of gasoline pumps mounted outside this "building" were the only discernible clues available to identify its purpose.

For many independents bold enough to differentiate themselves from the roadside norm, the gas station structure had become more than just a building to house an operator and cash register; it was a billboard in itself.

Changing of the Guard

By 1951, more than 50 million vehicles were on the road, with service station sales totaling $8.1 billion. Gasoline stations were big business, and the number of new operations opening to get their share of the wealth became overwhelming. The heavy saturation of the gasoline market that resulted brought about an atmosphere of competition seen only in the early days of the streetside pump.

With the number of stations escalating and competition increasing, the major oil companies changed their plans and decided to follow the initiative of the independents and their bold moves to revitalize gas station architecture. Most of the large oil concerns moved cautiously with minimal investment, redecorating the postwar

box by adding only simple architectural elements to its basic design. Some companies did choose to take radical steps, however, and drastically altered the look of their service stations in the postwar era.

Phillips Petroleum Company made a dramatic departure from its early house stations in the early fifties by adding a dramatic V-shaped roof rakishly angled toward the sky. Affixed to the office portion of a boxlike structure, it soared upward to be met at its apex by a three-tubed steel tower with exposed bracing. Piercing the pitched end of the canted wedge, the white tower held the familiar Phillips 66 shield high in the air. Beneath, long rows of neon tubing illuminated the wing in a dramatic spectacle of reflected light. Large angled windows installed in the office below highlighted automotive accesso-

Detail from the *Socony-Vacuum Drum Sales Station* manual. The distinctive Socony-Vacuum Mobilgas shield signs were either hung on a metal pole or mounted atop a fluted post at the outside corner of the new drum stations. *Courtesy Frederick G. Frost, Jr.*

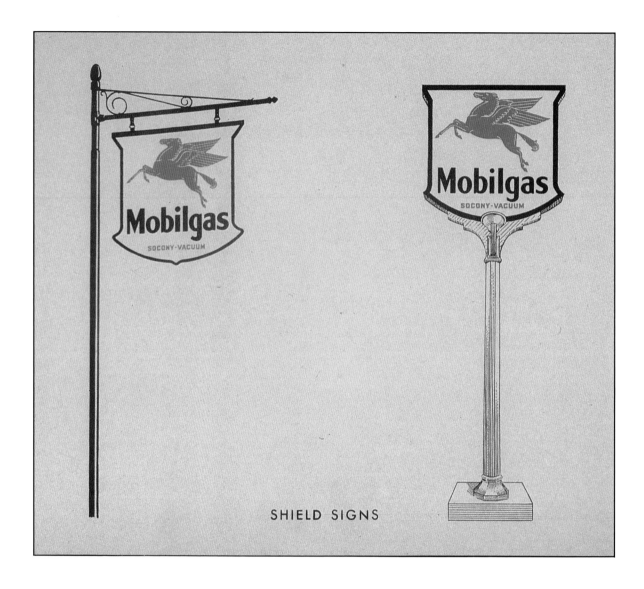

SHIELD SIGNS

ries behind jeweled facets. More like a space station than a gasoline refueling outlet, this structure with overblown features of the Exaggerated Modern Style endeavored to excite the senses of the passing motorist.

The canopy was changing in other ways too, as gigantic overhead structures began appearing at large multipump independent stations on the West Coast. Basically flat, they were a far cry from Phillips' exaggerated designs but easily made up in size what they lacked in excitement. Constructed entirely of steel bracing and sheet metal, they now covered everything on the lot—including the small station house

and gas pumps. Deep cornices allowed large lettering, company trademarks, slogans and advertising images to be mounted on all four sides, creating an oversized display guaranteed to attract attention.

With undersides finished in white enameled steel, the canopies often reflected light at a level equivalent to that of daylight. Flashlights weren't needed, as even an automobile engine could be examined without additional illumination. But that was only a side benefit of their installation. Canopies weren't built for practicality or protection from the elements; promotion was their primary duty. Designed for maximum nighttime

effect, they transformed an entire lot into a magnet for passing motorists. Any dimly lit service station with higher prices competing from across the street was hardly noticed.

The Urban Chameleon

Unfortunately, city planners and zoning authorities were watching, too. Cluttered and gaudy advertising, junkyard lots, outside storage of old tires, vending machines, telephone booths—all pointed toward an image problem getting out of hand. New station construction was soon banned in a number of cities as a storm of zoning regulations rained down on prospective entrepreneurs. With more and more unsuccessful operations forced out of business, abandoned structures were left to decay on the roadside. The community eyesores that resulted were unwanted by officials and reviled by the citizens who lived near them.

But unlike people in the twenties with their City Beautiful movement, ordinary citizens in the mid-sixties chose not to rally against the American gas station and its unfavorable image. This time, strong pressure from the White House effected the change. Beautification of the service station was led single-handedly by Mrs. Lyndon B. Johnson, an outspoken opponent of unregulated station construction. In a special Red Room meeting with twenty-seven oil marketers, she spoke convincingly about her desire to make service stations more attractive in 1966. Between sips of tea, oil company executives listened attentively.

With a full line of products to offer dealers and wholesalers, Phillips Petroleum Company expanded rapidly into the southeastern United States during the fifties. By then, tires, batteries and accessories first introduced into service station sales during the late twenties (to augment low revenues due to sagging fuel sales) had become an important part of sales for all the major oil companies. *Courtesy Phillips Petroleum Company*

Norman's Stafford Shell

*Out of these rusty cars and greasy floors
came great things. It sent our three kids
through college . . . now they're out there
helping people, helping society.*

Thirty years ago, Norman's Stafford Shell was
a busy gas station. In search of petroleum sus-
tenance, vehicles of all types flowed from a
single blacktop path into the station like hungry
insects. As benevolent keepers of the highway, Norman and Bertha Teitelbaum gladly
filled their tanks with the quenching distillate
known as gas and provided the simple services
once taken for granted. Service is our Business was only a slogan Shell Oil Company
used in those early days, but to the Teitelbaums it represented more than a catchy arrangement of words. The bright red letters emblazoned on their building meant a lifelong
commitment.

Back in the fifties when Norman's was in its
prime, US 1 was Gasoline Alley at its best and
home to hundreds of gas stations, diners and
special roadside attractions. In only a few
short miles of divided asphalt, a driver could
experience a multitude of sights and sounds
from the front seat of a moving automobile.
Slicing through the apple pie of Virginia's
countryside, this long stretch of highway in
Stafford County was a microcosm of the American dream.

But in the last thirty-plus years, things have
changed. The full-service gasoline stations
that were an important part of this once fre-
netic roadway have been transmogrified. The
traffic on US 1 has thinned as the eighteen-
wheelers that once provided its lifeblood roar
down 395, the Interstate freeway built over
twenty years ago to bypass it. The injustices of
time have erased practically all evidence of the
roadway's former character, completely altering its commerce. Traveling down this historic
ribbon of asphalt today, one can witness this
strange roadside metamorphosis in its final
throes.

Computerized self-service devices with their
sharp corners and sophisticated electronics
have replaced the streamlined pump and globe

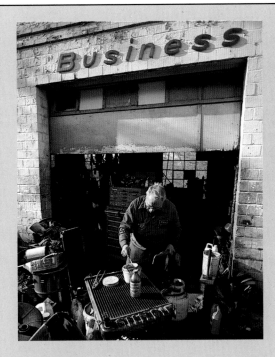

Norman keeps busy with an assortment of automotive-related tasks, including radiator repair. Though he doesn't pump gas anymore or provide drive-through services as he used to, he still believes in doing a job right the first time. It's a philosophy he has based his business upon.

Norman's Shell still has a working model of the ECO-brand Tireflator inflation units. Who could forget airing up bicycle and car tires at one of these beauties? Even with its case encrusted in heavy layers of peeling paint, it still conjures up happy memories of the classic American gas station. Twenty-five-cent air machines now standard at the neighborhood convenience store make one wonder why people ever took these Tireflator units for granted.

combination of yesteryear. Where air was once free, it's available for a quarter from a mechanized unit. Station attendants are securely positioned behind two inches of bulletproof glass, in touch with customers over a two-way intercom. Filthy restrooms are locked up tight; toilet paper theft and vandalism force customers to head back to the pay booth enclosure for the keys, along with the bowling ball attached to them to prevent their disappearance.

At Norman's, cars no longer pull in under their own power. Incapable of even the slightest locomotion, their rusted and wrecked remains arrive on the back of a tow truck. Like crushed gladiators returning from a lost battle, they sit defeated as part of the scrapyard in front of the station building. Many will be retired to a useless future of rust, others methodically cannibalized for parts. The lucky ones meet their final fate behind the station, past the house that the Teitelbaums have lived in for over twenty years now.

Back there, the impersonal jaws of the car crusher hold no grudges. Cadillac, DeSoto, Chevy, Volkswagen—their metal all bends in the same manner, easily compacting into the same handy block of scrap. Devoid of personality, the compressed alloys will be resold, then recycled. Reshaped into the pieces that will make up the next new car or toaster rolling off the assembly line, the nature of their existence will come full circle, just as Norman's has.

Every day, the Teitelbaums recycle remnants of former dreams to make way for new ones. The greasy floors and wrecked cars that make up their business constitute the financial firmament where the cash used to shape the lives of others originated. With revenues the station provided, all three of their children attended schools of higher learning and realized their personal dreams. As Bertha so aptly put it, "We worked with our hands so our children could work with their heads."

A recycling station for all of humanity, Norman's is making a slow return from the ashes. Like the phoenix, it rises, bringing life to others. In time, the hard work and supreme sacrifice the Teitelbaums have made will reap a multitude of extrinsic benefits for all of society. Bertha and Norman can be proud, as their junked cars have done more for humankind than they could ever know. Norman's Stafford Shell has become a place of rebirth, transcending into more than just a mere service station.

125

Matchbook covers were like miniature billboards where gasolines, motor oils, maintenance services and a variety of other wares could be advertised. Usually given away free to the customer, they were once a common sight at America's service station.

Sinclair Motor Oil's dinosaur stamp album of 1935 was just the right promotion to tie in with its company mascot, Dino. The weekly promotion stimulated the public's interest in paleontology. Twelve weekly visits to stations were necessary to collect all the stamps.
Atlantic Richfield Company

They already had plans in the works for new designs, though, and were merely letting the 95 million customers decide which type to commit to by monitoring sales. Not coincidentally, the rustic house design Shell Oil Company had pioneered in the fifties came out on top and became the new architectural direction that oil companies would inevitably take for their station buildings. Already anticipating the negative ground swell in advance, Shell had 3,500 of its Ranch Style service stations in place at the time of the Johnson gathering.

Teague's classic enameled stations—once considered beautiful in the thirties—and the genre of stations that imitated the style had lost favor with the public. Communities now bristled at the idea of oil companies erecting "refrigerators" in their neighborhoods. Not surprisingly, the oblong icebox was declared outmoded. The gasoline giants hastily converted their existing stations by adding clever "top hats" of front gable roofs. Cedar shingles, used brick and dark paint schemes were utilized to hide enameled steel and any hint of the rectangular. Cosmetic touches were added with hope that the service station box would finally blend into the streetside landscape.

Standard Oil Company of New York's Pegasus children's ride toured the country for new-station grand openings in the fifties. Like the coin-operated arcade horses found at amusement parlors and later shopping center walkways, they were powered by electric motor and gave a small child a quick ride in the "Old West" by way of their up and down rocking motion. Five of these portable units toured new openings around the country and were corralled at one specific stop for only a short period to facilitate maximum exposure and publicity.

1965

1954

1933

1911

The progression of the
Pegasus. Adopted as a
trademark in the United
States shortly after the organization of Socony-
Vacuum in 1931, the
symbol was used abroad as
long ago as 1911. South
Africa was the first to use
the Pegasus as a symbol of
speed and power. It was
Mobil Sekiyu in Japan,
however, that first colored
it red. *Courtesy Mobil
Corporation*

Company gargoyle, the White Eagle Petroleum Company White Eagle and the Mobil Flying Red Horse were all designed to entice the motorist.

Unfortunately, the continual rethinking of the gasoline station and the image it should portray caused many of these likable symbols to be tamed. The folksiness of yesterday's art was deemed too old-fashioned as the new advertising religion called for highly stylized images. Among the thousands of pictures vying for the public's attention every day, the superfluous were found to have no place. Marketing experts determined which colors and letters created the best impression for maximum gasoline sales, and psychologists analyzed trademarks for friendliness. Accepted emblems were suddenly rearranged in unfamiliar patterns of shapes and colors. By the seventies, some oil company symbols were so completely altered that they bore little resemblance to their earlier, more friendly, counterparts.

Mom and Pop Hang Up Their Hats

"A freeway is a strip of public land devoted to movement over which the abutting property owners have no right of light, air, or access [but] a motorist on the freeway will, of course, need supplies of all kinds, [such] as gasoline, oil, automobile parts, lunches, drugs, etc. . . . These may be obtained in freeway business centers placed in the middle of the freeway on small streets at intervals ranging from three to ten miles along the route. They will be so designed that the stores and filling stations are made invisible from the freeway by proper landscaping, and arranged so that access from the freeway will in no way interfere with the free flow of the traffic. No local access is provided for these business centers. They are for the exclusive use of the freeway travelers.
(Latham Squire and Howard Bassett, *American City* magazine, circa 1932)

The Interstate Highway Program authorized by Congress in 1956 threatened to change not only the way the public would travel, vacation and commute to work, but how and when they would purchase gasoline. Gobbling up huge tracts of land and marginally profitable service stations in the process, the construction called for the procurement of thousands of acres. With plans calling for 40,000 miles of four-lane roadways to link virtually ninety percent of all

This Ethyl magazine advertisement from 1949 was prepared in cooperation with "the specialists" of the American Museum of Natural History in New York as a handy guide to the trademarks of nature for young vacationers. The ad also sold gasoline for the seaside trip to Ma and Pa.

Next page top right
Forerunner to the modern gas station was this avant-garde design created by architect Frank Lloyd Wright and built in Cloquet, Minnesota. The design was based on a cantilever motif with the canopy extending 32 ft. out into space to shelter the L-shaped gas pumps. The office mimicked an airport control tower, and the roof was sheathed in copper.

cities in the United States, construction was quickly started in 1957. A total 26,500 miles of interstate routes were scheduled for completion by the late sixties, affecting thousands of gas outlets already in operation. By the mid-seventies, towns with populations over 30,000 would have access to the new regional system.

Many smaller towns were avoided by the path of the "highway revolution" and became sealed off from the main flow of cross-country traffic. Without access roads spaced at realistic intervals to allow motorists to impulsively pull over and patronize a business that looked good, frequently a vehicle could not stop. Exiting the fast pace of the freeway had to be thought out and planned miles in advance. Isolated from the new speedways by tracts of grass and fencing, motels, cafes, souvenir shops and gas stations were left to wither. Thriving communities be-

Intersection Highway 33 and Cloquet Ave.
Cloquet, Minn.

In the wake of Mrs. Lyndon B. Johnson's 1966 meeting on how to make the gasoline station more beautiful, oil companies such as Shell fully implemented their plans for the Ranch-Style station buildings first introduced in the fifties in the hope of blending the business of selling gasoline into the landscape. Utilizing architectural elements such as used brick, rustic wood and stone to achieve the look, the approach took into consideration any landscaping existing at the station site. *Shell Oil Company*

came virtual ghost towns overnight as vast stretches of two-lane highway once packed with traffic lost the trade of motorists now flying past on the new interstates. Commercial business strips alive with life only months earlier were abandoned.

By 1972, the gasoline stations that had somehow survived the restructuring of America's roadways were faced with another pressing problem: Would they get the gasoline supplies they needed at prices that allowed them to make a profit and keep their establishments open, or would they be forced out of business? When gas trucks failed to deliver new supplies and underground tanks ran dry, the answer became clear. The OPEC oil embargo was making a dramatic impact on the gasoline station and hampering motorists' ability to purchase fuel. Imports of precious crude were severely limited while current reserves were reported to be inadequate.

Three percent of all fuel was allocated for emergency use, and commercial customers were allowed 100 percent of current requirements; agricultural, communications and municipal services received their full allotments, too. Whatever gasoline supply remained was to be equitably distributed among the thousands of retail outlets, both independent and company owned.

As a result of the so-called gas shortage, one Denver station operator received only sixty percent of the gasoline he needed from his supplier. Some stations got even less, if any. Without enough fuel supplies to turn a profit, thousands of marginally profitable gas businesses were effectively shut down. By the end of 1973, five percent of the 218,000 gas stations in business when the year began had closed their doors.

Industry analysts predicted that within the next six months, the independent mom-and-pop gasoline filling station would be rendered obsolete. The hierarchy of fuel distribution, priority deliveries to company stations and increased competition had forced many independent operators out of business. Selling the liquid that kept an entire population on the move became a more difficult prospect than it ever had been in the history of gasoline marketing. Change was inevitable, and without any further recourse, more than 10,000 gasoline stations of all types were closed down, sold, demolished or abandoned.

Previous page
Designed as the new standard for Mobil stations worldwide, the Pegasus station design originated by well-known architect Eliot Noyes contained round canopies, cylindrical pumps and bold "minimal" signage. While other oil companies were trying to disguise the service station with environmental motifs during the mid-sixties, Mobile went against the pack and constructed many of these "less-is-more" stations. The circular design of the new structures gave Mobil a unique and instantly recognizable identity in the marketplace overbuilt with "suburban" styles. *Courtesy Mobil Corporation*

Otto Sorenson, proud owner, mechanic and gas attendant at Sorenson & Sons full-service gas station in Graham, Washington. By the nineties, the full-service station was largely a thing of the past. Sorenson does it all, however—and always with a smile!

The Mazama Country Store
in eastern Washington
State. In the current days of
superstations, this little gas
station and general store
still ekes out an existence,
complete with an ancient
visible-register gas pump.

Last Chance Gas: Learning From Route 66

The old stretches of asphalt once alive with traffic along the National Road, Route 66 and Lincoln Highway have now grown quiet. Today, the remnants of old gas pumps and abandoned station buildings sit empty—silent, waiting. The rust and corrosion of the years slowly engulf their exteriors with a heavy patina of time. Like faded billboards, they have lost their original meaning. A new era of gasoline superstation has arrived, the golden age of "wipe the windows and check the oil" has ended.

A slow metamorphosis has taken place, expediting this partial transition into oblivion. The helpful attitudes and friendly customs once an integral part of the service station of yesterday have been altered by the attitudes of society. Today, *service* has a new definition: Do it yourself! Repair garages and mechanics once taken for granted have been virtually eliminated from the modern gasoline establishment. Gone are the days of the free glass giveaways and premium offers. High-volume pumpers have filled the void, offering everything from cheap, folding sunglasses to Pudding Pops in their pricey mini-markets. Technological advances have made it easier for twentieth-century people to fill their tank, stuff their face and empty their pocketbook.

Like so many other icons of Americana, the once classic service station has mutated into a new form. Now, only remnants of what it was dot the highways. A rusting gas pump is usually all that remains. Symbolizing another era, another way of life, these retired pumpers represent values that have since eroded. With an ethereal character all their own, they decay in glory—tombstones of the past. Transformed, aesthetic attitudes of former generations permeate their every molecule. Worn out by a society faithfully served, they measure the advancement of change as roadside barometers.

Whether altered by the elements, the station owner with spray paint or the vandal wielding a hammer, these "sculptures of use" have opened windows to another dimension. Yet at any moment, the floods of change could widen the stream and eliminate all the environmental art that has come into creation streetside. From the roadside shoulder, we watch the rushing currents of time wash over our most cherished institutions. With the onslaught of new shopping malls, parking lots and wider streets, the valuable links to the past are quickly being eradicated. Soon, the surrealistic signposts that constitute this country's vernacular roadside and make it truly American will vanish forever.

Gas Pump Graveyard
Discarded pumps create an echo of the real graveyard in the distance behind them, right across the street. Now even the calculator pumps once considered modern are discarded as yesterday's old technology. The age of the computer is upon us, changing the way we purchase gas.

"Let Us Check Your Oil"
Now part of an unused oil can dispenser installed on the tattered gas island in front of Norman's Stafford Shell in Falmouth, the broken glass of this Let us check your oil for safety placard sets up an ironic interplay of images. Even so, Norman's still serves a valuable function by supplying the used parts needed to keep automobiles running.

Last Chance Gas
One last place for fuel on the side of the roadway along US 67, this desolate refueling station in Venus, Texas, awaits its final customer.

Quicker Starting
Super Union Gasoline poster and advertisement, circa 1930.

Tailpipes
The collective mileage seen by these discarded mufflers near Ellensburg, Washington, could easily wrap many times around the earth. All required gasoline to get where they were going and helped keep thousands of gasoline stations in business.

"Fresh Up" With 7–Up
This sign is a roadside survivor from the days when advertising messages were simple and to the point. Now, Madison Avenue bombards the motorist with tremendous billboards of cola-swigging celebrities, choosing to eliminate the friendly messages of yesteryear.

Rose Street Auto Repair
Inside the office of Rose Street Auto Repair in Seattle, one can witness the classic view from Wally Hilde's service station office. All the standard elements that should be found are in their proper place, including humorous signs and pinup calendar. Today, *People* magazine and breath mints obscure the view from behind the typical convenience market cash register.

One for the Road
Familiar Coke signs remain intact on this decaying Gulf station and food stop located in Caddomilles, Texas.

148

Hoser Out of Gas
Near the stockyards area of Fort Worth, Texas, stands this unit. The station it once served is out of business.

Three Tokheim pumps do a ritual dance outside this gas-crunched station in Colorado Springs.

Food, Gas
A combination "hot dog" lunchroom and service station now sits abandoned in Cle Ellum, Washington. The high-priced convenience mart and fast-food hamburger franchise have replaced the mom-and-pop snack bar business.

General Store
The old-time store and gas station closed for business a long time ago off Highway 647 in Lignum, Virginia.

Rest Room
The Registered Rest Room—a Texaco promotion—was an idea that didn't last long in the business of this gas station near Las Vegas, Nevada.

153

Furrer's Pump
Completely stripped and vandalized, this pump unit in Picacho Peak, Arizona, has now become the object of many people's anger. When you're down and out, friends are hard to come by.

Under New Management
The gas pumps remaining on the roadside along I–35 in Oklahoma stand as reminders to the way things were, the values and service of yesterday. When they are all gone, what will remain to remind us of the way things were?

Bibliography

Anderson, Scott. *Check the Oil: Gas Station Collectibles with Prices.* Pittsburgh: Wallace-Homestead Book Co., 1986.

Anderson, Warren H. *Vanishing Roadside America.* Tucson, AZ.: University of Arizona Press, 1981.

Anderson, Will. *Mid-Atlantic Roadside Delights.* Portland, ME: Anderson & Sons Publishing Co., 1991.

———. *New England Roadside Delights.* Portland, ME: Anderson & Sons Publishing Co., 1989.

Baeder, John. *Gas, Food and Lodging: A Postcard Odyssey through the Great American Roadside.* New York: Abbeville Press, 1982.

"Baker Oil Company Presents Extensive New Calsteel Built Service Facility." *Gas Station and Garage* 34 (May 1950) : 10.

Bayer, Patricia. *Art Deco Sourcebook.* Secaucus, NJ: Wellfleet Press, 1988.

Beaton, Kendall. *Enterprise in Oil.* New York: Appleton-Century-Crofts, 1957.

Bogstahl, Mars. "Storm Warnings Up for Stations." *National Petroleum News* 56 (July 1964) : 103–106.

Boyne, Walter J. *Power behind the Wheel: Creativity and Evolution of the Automobile.* New York: Stewart, Tabori & Chang, 1988.

A Brief History of Mobil. Fairfax, VA.: Mobil Corporation, 1991.

"By-pass Highways for Traffic Relief." *American City* 38 (April 1928) : 88–90.

"Calcor Built Neighborhood Station Features Complete Service for Every Car." *Gas Station and Garage* 34 (February 1950) : 8.

"Canopies: What's behind an Old Standby's New Appeal." *National Petroleum News* 50 (November 1958) : 99–104.

Chaffee, Wib. "What Is a 'Super Service' Station?" *Automobile Digest* (February 1929) : 12–13, 68–70.

"Changes at the Pump." *Time* 86 (July 9, 1965) : 90.

Coate, Roland E. "An Auto Service Station." *Architectural Record* 63 (April 1928) : 303.

Crosser, C. A. "Curbing the Curb Pump." *American City* 29 (August 1923) : 155–156.

Dale, Craig. "Is Main Street Doomed?" *Popular Mechanics* 55 (May 1931) : 756–768.

"A Detour for Roadside America." *Business Week* (February 16, 1974) : 44.

"Does Beauty Sell? Mobil Tries to Find Out." *National Petroleum News* 58 (November 1966) : 120.

"Down They Come." *Standard Oil Bulletin* 11 (March 1924) : 3.

Draper, George O. "A View of the Tour from One Participating." *Horseless Age* 16 (July 26, 1905) : 153.

Edmond, Mark. "What Marketers Are Doing—or Not Doing—about Closed Stations." *National Petroleum News* 64 (April 1972) : 82–85.

"Elevating the Standing of the 'Hot Dog Kennel.'" *American City* 38 (May 1928) : 99–100.

Elwell, Richard R. "California Is Off Again, As . . . Multipumps Revive the Canopy." *National Petroleum News* 47 (November 1955) : 41–42.

"Filling Stations as Embryo Cities." *Literary Digest* 107 (November 29, 1930) : 44.

Flink, James J. *The Automobile Age.* Cambridge, MA: M.I.T. Press, 1988.

Frazer, Elizabeth. "The Destruction of Rural America: Game, Fish and Flower Hogs." *The Saturday Evening Post* (May 9, 1929) : 39, 193–194, 197–198.

"'Gas-A-Terias': Self-served Gasoline Saves a Nickel a

Gallon for California Drivers." *Life* 25 (November 22, 1948) : 129.

"Gasoline: Help Yourself Boom." *Newsweek* 30 (December 29, 1947) : 48.

"Gasoline: War against Self-service." *Newsweek* 33 (April 25, 1949) : 69-70.

Gasoline Pump Manufacturers Association. *Gasoline Pump Blue Book.* New York: 1952.

"Gasoline Stations Become Architectural Assets." *American City* 41 (November 1929) : 98-99.

Gelderman, Carol. *Henry Ford: The Wayward Capitalist.* New York: St. Martin's Press, 1981.

Hastings, Charles Warren. "Roadtown, the Linear City." *Architects and Builders Magazine* 10 (August 1910) : 445.

Helen, Christine Bennett. " 'Pinkie's Pantry' Took the Cake." *American Magazine* (June 1928) : 65-66.

Hocke, John. "An Up-to-date Greasing Palace." *American Builder and Building Age* 52 (December 1930) : 80-81.

Hokansen, Drake. *The Lincoln Highway: Main Street across America.* Iowa City, IA: University of Iowa Press, 1988.

"How Ranch Style Is Taking Over Service-Station Design." *National Petroleum News* 58 (May 1966) : 95-101.

Hungerford, Edward. "America Awheel." *Everybody's Magazine* 36 (June 1917) : 678.

Jakle, John A. "The American Gasoline Station, 1920-1970." *Journal of American Culture* 1 (Spring 1978) : 520-542.

James, Marquis. *The Texaco Story: The First Fifty Years, 1902-1952.* New York: Texas Co., 1953.

Jones, Charles L. *Service Station Management: Its Principles and Practice.* New York: D. Van Nostrand Co., 1922.

Jordan, Michael. "Lost in the Fifties." *Automobile Magazine* (November 1988) : 123-125.

Keller, Ulrich. *The Highway as Habitat: A Roy Stryker Documentation, 1943-1955.* Santa Barbara, CA: University Art Museum, 1986.

Kerouac, Jack. *On the Road.* New York: Viking Penguin, 1955.

Knowles, Ruth Sheldon. *The First Pictorial History of the American Oil and Gas Industry, 1859-1983.* Athens, OH: Ohio University Press, 1983.

Kowinski, William Severini. "Suburbia: End of the Golden Age." *New York Times Magazine* (March 16, 1980) : 16-19, 106.

Kuntz, J. F. "Greek Architecture and Gasoline Service Stations." *American City* 27 (August 1922) : 123-124.

Langdon, Philip. *Orange Roofs, Golden Arches: The Architecture of American Chain Restaurants.* New York: Alfred A. Knopf, 1986.

Lay, Charles Downing. "New Towns for High-Speed Roads." *Architectural Record* 78 (November 1935) : 352-354.

Lee, Bob. *Tokheim Pump Company: An Illustrated History.* Detroit, MI: Harlo Press, 1980.

Liebs, Chester. *Main Street to Miracle Mile: American Roadside Architecture.* Boston: Little, Brown & Co., 1985.

"Life after Death along Gasoline Alley." *Fortune* (November 5, 1979) : 86-89.

Link, Joe. "Attacks on Service Stations Mount while Oil Remains Silent." *National Petroleum News* 64 (March 1972) : 46-48.

Lohof, Bruce A. "The Service Station in America: The Evolution of a Vernacular Form." *Industrial Archeology* 11 (1974) : 1-13.

Londberg-Holm, K. "The Gasoline Filling and Service Station." *Architectural Record* 67 (June 1930): 563-571.

Love, Ed. *Gas and Oil Trademarks:hVolume 2.* Colorado Springs, CO: Villa Publishing Syndicate, 1990.

———.*United States Design Patents: Series 1.* Colorado Springs, CO: Villa Publishing Syndicate, 1990.

———, and Larry T. Drivas. *Gas and Oil Trademarks: Volume 1.* Colorago Springs, CO: Villa Publishing Syndicate, 1988.

Lowe, Lucy. "Service Stations as an Asset to the City." *American City* 25 (August 1921) : 151-153.

Mackaye, Benton, and Lewis Mumford. "Townless Highways for the Motorist." *Harper's* 163 (August 1931) : 347-356.

Margolies, John. *The End of the Road: Vanishing Highway Architecture in America.* New York: Viking Press, 1981.

Marling, Karal Ann. *The Colossus of Roads: Myth and Symbol along the American Highway.* Minneapolis, MN: University of Minnesota Press, 1984.

McCabe, Axe, and Ed Love. *Gas Stations and Related Designs: Volume 1.* Colorado Springs, CO: Villa Publishing Syndicate, 1989.

———. *Gas Stations and Related Designs: Volume 3.* Colorado Springs, CO: Villa Publishing Syndicate, 1990.

Mills, Joseph E. *Garage Management and Control.* New York: A. W. Shaw Co., 1928.

Minnick, Richard G. "The Silent Sentinel of the American Road—Part 1." *Antique Automobile* (January 1964) : 17-27.

"Money to Be Made: The Oil Marketing Story." *National Petroleum News* 61 (February 1969) : 111-130.

Moore, Stanley T. "Individual Service Station Design." *National Petroleum News* 25 (June 14, 1933) : 53-57.

"Motorists Tell in Their Own Words What They Expect at Filling Stations." *National Petroleum News* (November 17, 1926) : 92.

National Trust for Historic Preservation. *Ducks and Diners*. Edited by Diane Maddex and Janet Walker. Washington, D.C.: Preservation Press, 1988.

"New Life for Old Stations." *National Petroleum News* 56 (September 1964) : 101-104.

Oppel, Frank. *Motoring in America: The Early Years*. Secaucus, NJ: Castle Books, 1989.

Partridge, Bellamy. *Fill 'er Up!* Reprint. Los Angeles: Floyd Clymer, 1959.

Patton, Phil. *Open Road: A Celebration of the American Highway*. New York: Simon & Schuster, 1986.

Phillips Petroleum Co. *Phillips: The First Sixty-six Years*. Edited by William C. Wertz. Phillips Petroleum Co., 1983. A public affairs publication.

———. *Why Sixty-six?* Bartlesville, OK.: 1991.

Platt, Warren C. "Competition Invited by the Nature of the Oil Industry." *National Petroleum News* (February 5, 1936) : 205.

"Prototype for Service Stations: Mobil Tests Effect of Design on Sales at Fifty-eight Locations." *Architectural Record* 141 (May 1967) : 172-175.

"Prototype Gas Station Looks Like a Winner—and Is." *Progressive Achitecture* 53 (October 1972) : 31.

"Pump's Progress—The Tower to Match the Power." *Texaco Dealer* (February 1958) : 8-10.

Reid, Marvin. "The Sophisticated Self-serve Comes of Age, Part I: Self-serves and C-stores." *National Petroleum News* 69 (July 1977) : 54-63.

Ridder, Holger. "Stations Become Merchandising Tools for Boosting Sales, Giving Better Service." *National Petroleum News* (March 29, 1950) : 26-40.

Ripp, Bart. "All Pumped Up." *Tacoma News Tribune* (July 25, 1989).

Rowsome, Frank, Jr. *The Verse by the Side of the Road*. MA: Stephen Greene Press, 1965.

"Scenic or Sign-ic?" *Standard Oil Bulletin* 17 (September 1929) : 14-16.

Schroeder, Richard C. "How and When to Modernize Your Service Stations." *National Petroleum News* 50 (October 1958) : 84-89.

Scott, Quinta. *Route 66: The Highway and Its People*. Norman, OK: University of Oklahoma Press, 1988.

Sculle, Keith A. "C. A. Petersen: Pioneer Gas Station Architect." *Historic Illinois* 2 (June 1979) : 11-13.

———. "The Vernacular Gasoline Station: Examples from Illinois and Wisconsin." *Journal of Cultural Geography* 1 (Spring-Summer 1981): 56-74.

"Self-service Moves In on the Pump." *Business Week* (October 1, 1966) : 129-130.

"Self-service Stations: New Marketing Pattern?" *Business Week* (July 24, 1948) : 68.

"Service-Station Beautification Is Coming in for Ever-Increasing Attention." *National Petroleum News* 58 (March 1966) : 81-82.

"Service-Station Design." *National Petroleum News* 42 (March 29, 1950) : 30.

"Service Stations." *Architectural Record* 97 (February 1944) : 71-92.

"Service Stations: The Needless Blot." *Fortune* 74 (September 1966) : 159-160.

"Shell Oil's Newest 'Blend-in.'" *National Petroleum News* 52 (February 1960) : 121.

Silk, Gerald, et al. *Automobile and Culture*. New York: Harry N. Abrams, 1984.

Sinclair Oil Corp. *A Great Name in Oil: Sinclair through Fifty Years*. Editorial consultant, Hartzell Spence. New York: F. W. Dodge Co. and McGraw-Hill, 1966.

Society for Commercial Archeology. *The Automobile in Design and Culture*. Edited by Jan Jennings. Ames, IA: Iowa State University Press, 1990.

Squire, Latham C., and Howard M. Bassett. "A New Type of Thoroughfare: The 'Freeway.'" *American City* 47 (November 1932) : 64-66.

"Staebler Opens Modern Station in Ann Arbor." *National Petroleum News* 25 (May 31, 1933) : 34.

"Standardized Service Stations Designed by Walter Dorwin Teague." *Architectural Record* 82 (September 1937) : 69-72.

Stern, Jane, and Michael Stern. *Road Food*. New York: Random House, 1980.

Stern, Rudi. *Let There Be Neon*. New York: Harry N. Abrams, 1979.

"Super Service Station: A Plan for a Corner Lot." *Automobile Digest* 17 (January 1929) : 37.

Sweeney, Don. "California's Self Service Stations Still in Limelight." *National Petroleum News* 40 (May 25, 1948) : 9.

———. "New Stations Designed to Stress Eye Appeal in Pushing the Sale of TBA." *National Petroleum News* 40 (January 14, 1948) : 36-37.

Teague, Walter Dorwin. *Design This Day: The Technique of Order in the Machine Age*. New York: Harcourt, Brace & Co., 1940.

Thomas, Diane C. "Lonely Road Now." *Atlanta Magazine* (November 1978) : 57-59, 123-124.

Thompson, Craig. *Since Spindletop: A Human Story of Gulf's First Half-Century*. Pittsburgh: Gulf Oil Corp., 1951.

"Tokheim Corporation: Poised for a Gas Pump Boom."

Dun's Review (October 1979) : 20–25.

"Tomorrow's Gas Station." *Popular Science* 149 (November 1946) : 100–101.

"Travel Service with a Twist." *National Petroleum News* 52 (February 1960) : 118.

"Treads and Threads." *Time* (October 12, 1981) : 72.

"Vacancies on Gasoline Alley." *Business Week* (December 15, 1953) ; 20–21.

Veeder-Root Co. *Twenty Years of Development.* Hartford, CT: 1991.

Vieyra, Daniel I. *"Fill 'er Up": An Architectural History of America's Gas Stations.* New York: Collier Macmillan Publishers, 1979.

Von Eckardt, Wolf. "Toward a Better Community: Must Gas Stations Be Garish?" *American Home* (June 1967) : 40–41.

Wallis, Michael. *Route 66: The Mother Road.* New York: St. Martin's Press, 1990.

Walton, Richard J. *The Power of Oil.* New York: Seabury Press, 1977.

"Wayside Stands, Billboards, Curb Pumps, Lunch Wagons, Junk Yards and Their Ilk." *American City* 44 (April 1931) : 104–108.

"Who'll Get Helped or Hurt by Auto Freeways?" *U.S. News and World Report* (December 21, 1956) : 90–92.

Wilson, Richard Guy, Dianne H. Pilgrim and Dickran Tashjian. *The Machine Age in America, 1918–1941.* New York: Harry N. Abrams, 1986.

Woodson, LeRoy. *Roadside Food.* New York: Stewart, Tabori & Chang, 1986.

Index